AF661942

CONTINENTAL COOKING

FOR THE INDIAN PALATE

OTHER LOTUS TITLES

IT Cookbook
Street Foods of India
The Landour Cookbook
Nutritive Cooking for Children
Moti Mahal's Tandoori Trail
The Indian Vegetarian Cookbook

CHEFS' SPECIAL SERIES

Awadhi Kitchen
Bengali Kitchen
Chinese Kitchen
Chicken Delight
Curries and Rice
Delhi Kitchen
Dum Cuisine
Favourite Indian Desserts
Goan Kitchen
Gujarati Kitchen
Iyer Kitchen
Kerala Kitchen
Kashmiri Kitchen
Low Calorie Desserts
Marwari Kitchen
Nepalese Kitchen
Punjabi Kitchen
Parsi Kitchen
Rajasthani Kitchen
Seafood Platter
Snacks and Desserts
South Indian Kitchen
Thai Kitchen
Tikkas and Kebabs
Vegetarian Fiesta

CONTINENTAL COOKING
FOR THE INDIAN PALATE

CHAND SUR

LOTUS COLLECTION
ROLI BOOKS

In loving memory of my husband, Inder Sur

Lotus Collection
© Roli Books 2003

All rights reserved. No part of this publication may be reproduced or transmitted, in any form or by any means, without the prior permission of the publisher.

First published in 2003
Second impression 2010
Lotus Collection
An imprint of Roli Books Pvt. Ltd.
M-75, G.K. II Market, New Delhi 110 048
Phones: ++91-011-2921 2271, 40682000. Fax: ++91 (011) 2921 7185
E-mail: info@rolibooks.com; Website: www.rolibooks.com
Also at Bangalore, Chennai, Jaipur, Kolkata & Mumbai

Design: Supriya Saran

ISBN: 978-81-7436-269-8

Typeset in Arno Pro by Roli Books Pvt. Ltd.
and printed at Excel Printers Pvt. Ltd., Naraina, New Delhi

CONTENTS

ACKNOWLEDGEMENTS

My special thanks to my elder daughter, Sunita Kohli, who persuaded and encouraged me to write this book. My thanks to Shuchi and Ashok Sur and the rest of my family who have been supportive and helpful.

FLAVOURS OF INDIAN CONTINENT(AL)

Food prepared and served with care and eaten with relish is one of life's great pleasures. In this book, I have tried to provide continental dishes to suit the Indian palate, and used the most familiar ingredients that are available even in small cities. I have tried to find suitable substitutes for herbs and exotic vegetables native to the West in my recipes.

A good cook never scorns simple inexpensive foods, but gives them an interesting look, for the appearance of a dish is every bit as important as its vitamin content and its flavour. It is the appeal to the eye that tempts the appetite. The simplest garnish will transform an otherwise ordinary meal into a sumptuous repast. Anyone can be a good cook by devoting time and care to the preparation of food and being fairly critical about the finished product. The food you buy is very important: in other words shop carefully and wisely and try to use the freshest ingredients.

I hope you will enjoy working with me via this book.

BASIC RECIPES

Chicken Stock: Take the neck, backbone and bones of the chicken, ½ medium-sized onion, chopped; ¼″ginger, chopped; 8-10 black peppercorns; and 1 medium-sized carrot, cut lengthwise.

Boil the chicken bones in 3-4 cups water. Remove the scum. Add all the ingredients and pressure cook for 5-10 minutes. Then lower heat and cook for half an hour. Strain and add salt to taste. Use as required.

Fish Stock: Take fish bones and trimmings, washed; 4½ cups cold water; 1 onion, skinned and sliced, and bouquet garni (a bunch of herbs).

Put the fish in a pan, cover with water and add a little salt. Bring to the boil and remove any scum. Reduce heat and add the onion and bouquet garni. Cover, simmer for 20 minutes and strain. Use as required.

Vegetable Broth: Take 3 cups mixed vegetables, 3 tbsp butter, and 4 cups boiling water or part water and tomato juice.

Sauté the vegetables gently in butter. Do not brown them. Add boiling water or part water and tomato juice and simmer, partially covered, for about 1 hour. Season to taste. Use as required.

VARIOUS METHODS OF COOKING MEAT

Boil: This method is used for large pieces of meat or joints. Place the fresh meat in boiling water; bring the water back to the boil, then simmer until the meat is tender.

Braise: Cook slowly in a tightly covered casserole, with a small quantity of water or stock at 150°C / 300°F in the oven.

Deep Fat Frying: Cook in hot fat, deep enough to cover the meat in the pan.

Fricassee: Stew of white meat or poultry served in white sauce.

Grill or Broil: This method is suitable for cutlets, steaks, chops, kidneys, and so on. Wipe the meat, trim off surplus fat, season and brush with oil or melted fat. Grease and heat the grill before placing the meat over it.

Pot Roast: A piece of meat cooked slowly in a covered dish on a stove top.

Roast: Stand meat on a grill in a baking tin and roast in a hot oven (180°C / 350°F), basting with butter or drippings from time to time.

Sauté: To cook in an open pan in hot, shallow fat, tossing the food to prevent it from sticking.

Sear: Cook meat in intense heat to seal in the juices.

Shallow-fry: Meat fried in a small quantity of fat.

Simmer: To boil gently on low heat.

Skewer: Fasten together pieces of food compactly on a specially designed long pin, for cooking.

Steam: To cook food in steam. Generally, food to be steamed is put in a perforated container which is placed above a pan of boiling water. The food should not come into contact with the water.

Stew: To cook the food slowly in a tightly covered casserole, in a small quantity of liquid at low temperature.

Note: Frozen meat of any kind must never be put in hot water to thaw as it only toughens the flesh. Meat that has to be thawed quickly can be put under cool, running water.

SELECTING MEAT

Lamb: The flesh of lamb is a pale rose colour and has firm pearly white fat; it should feel firm to the touch. If it is flabby, it will be flavourless.

Mutton: Good mutton is a deeper pink, almost red and has large bones. The meat is plump without being over fat. The flesh should be firm and the fat thick and waxy in texture. Cooking time for mutton is longer than lamb.

Chicken: It is very important when selecting poultry to be able to tell whether a bird is young or old. Chicken should never have a gamey smell, however slight. When young, the legs and comb are smooth; when old, rough. The bird should be plump on the breast, fat on the back and have pliable feet.

The popular types of chicken used for cooking are:
Baby Chicken: (Poussin) 4-6 weeks old. Allow one poussin per person. Suitable for grilling and roasting.

Broiler: 8 -10 weeks old and serves four. Suitable for roasting, frying, grilling or baking.

Boiling Fowl: This is an older bird, usually a hen, and is suitable for boiling, stews, and casseroles.

Fish: Always be careful and check for freshness when buying fish. The flesh should be firm and the eyes bright, with no unpleasant smell.

There are many ways in which fish is cooked:

Bake: Bake the fish covered in a moderately hot oven (180°C / 350°F) with a little seasoned butter, placed on greased paper, using stock or milk to keep it moist. If you want the fish to brown slightly on top, leave the dish uncovered.

Fry: There are two basic ways of frying fish; in shallow fat or oil, or in deep fat or oil.

If shallow-frying the fish then only a small quantity of fat is used, in a shallow pan. The food must be turned halfway through to cook both sides.

If deep-frying the fish sufficient fat is used to cover the food completely in a deep pan. The cooking time is a little shorter when deep-frying than shallow-frying.

Grill: The grill should be really hot before putting the fish under it. The grid of the grill should be well-greased and the fish basted from time to time to prevent drying.

Poach: To cook gently in an open pan, either in salted water or in a fish stock. Never boil fish rapidly. It will break and become dry.

CHICKEN

CHICKEN WITH SPAGHETTI AND MUSHROOMS

PREPARATION TIME: 10 MIN.
COOKING TIME: 30 MIN.
SERVES: 6

Ingredients

100 gm Spaghetti
1 kg Chicken, broiler
Salt to taste
2-3 Carrots (*gajar*), medium-sized, chopped
2 Onions, medium-sized, chopped
3-4 Cloves (*laung*)
a few Black peppercorns (*sabut kali mirch*)
2-3 Celery, chopped
2 Green chillies, whole

For the sauce
3 tbsp / 60 gm Butter
2 tbsp / 20 gm Refined flour (*maida*)
150 gm Mushrooms, chopped
2 tbsp / 40 ml Cream

Method

- Cook the chicken with salt, carrots, onions, cloves, black peppercorns, celery, and green chillies in 5 cups of water in a pressure cooker. After about 10 minutes or when cooked, remove from heat. Take the chicken out and keep aside to cool.
- When cool, debone the chicken and dice into pieces. Put the bones

back into the pressure cooker and cook for 5-10 minutes on low heat. Now strain the stock and keep aside.

- Boil the spaghetti in enough water to cover and when soft, drain in cold water to prevent it from clumping.
- For the sauce, melt 2 tbsp butter in a saucepan. Add the flour and sauté for a minute till it browns slightly and bubbles appear. Remove from heat and make a smooth sauce, by gradually adding 2½ cups of chicken stock.
- Heat 1 tbsp butter in another saucepan; sauté the mushrooms. Add salt and pepper.
- To the prepared sauce, add the diced chicken, spaghetti, mushrooms, and cream. Toss and serve. To make it spicy, add a little Tabasco or chilli sauce to taste.

RUB AND SNIFF

RUB CHICKEN WITH TURMERIC POWDER AND KEEP FOR A FEW MINUTES BEFORE WASHING TO GET RID OF ANY PECULIAR SMELL IT MIGHT HAVE.

CHICKEN WITH MUSHROOMS

PREPARATION TIME: 10 MIN.
COOKING TIME: 30 MIN.
SERVES: 4

Ingredients

1 kg Chicken, boneless
150 gm Mushrooms, sliced
1 Onion, large, chopped
2 Green chillies, whole
10 Black peppercorns (*sabut kali mirch*)
Salt to taste
2 Bay leaves (*tej patta*)
4 tbsp / 80 gm Butter, melted
2 tbsp / 20 gm Refined flour (*maida*)
1 cup / 200 ml Milk
3 cups / 600 ml Chicken stock (see p. 9)
a little Cream
Salt to taste
Slices of bread, toasted or fried, cut into triangles for garnishing

Method

- Pressure cook or steam the chicken with giblets, onion, green chillies, black peppercorns, salt, and bay leaves. When done, remove and dice.
- In the same liquid in which the chicken was cooked, add the chicken bones and cook for five minutes more on low heat. Strain the stock and keep aside.
- Heat two tbsp butter in a pan; add the flour and sauté for a couple of minutes. Remove the pan from the heat; gradually add the chicken stock and milk. Mix continuously until smooth.
- Add the diced chicken, return the pan to the heat and cook gently for 15 minutes.
- Meanwhile, heat the remaining butter in a separate pan and sauté the mushrooms till soft. Remove and add the mushrooms, cream, and salt into the chicken mixture.
- Serve hot garnished with fried or toasted slices of bread.

FRIED CHICKEN

PREPARATION TIME: 5 MIN.
COOKING TIME: 20 MIN.
SERVES: 2

Ingredients

2 Chickens, broilers, wings, breasts
Salt to taste
1 tbsp / 10 gm Refined flour (*maida*)
½ tsp / 1 gm Black pepper (*kali mirch*), freshly ground
2 Eggs, beaten
1 cup / 120 gm Breadcrumbs
4-6 Tomatoes, medium-sized, halved

Method

- With the blunt side of a knife beat the chicken pieces on both sides; apply salt and keep aside.
- Mix the flour, salt, and black pepper together. Dust both sides of the chicken with this mixture.
- Heat the oil in a frying pan; dip the chicken in egg, coat with breadcrumbs and shallow-fry till tender. Remove and drain the excess oil on paper towels. Repeat with the other pieces.
- In the same pan, fry the tomatoes till soft.
- Serve the fried chicken with the tomatoes.

SKEWERED CHICKEN AND LIVER

PREPARATION TIME: 2 HRS.
COOKING TIME: 30 MIN.
SERVES: 4

Ingredients

4 Chicken breasts, boneless, cut into cubes
250 gm Liver, skin removed, cubed
10 Garlic (*lasan*) cloves
1 Ginger (*adrak*), 1" piece
Salt to taste
a big pinch Red chilli powder
2 tbsp / 30 ml Refined oil

Method

- Grind the garlic and ginger together; squeeze out the juice and keep aside.
- Marinate the chicken and liver in the garlic and ginger juice, salt, and red chilli powder for about two hours.
- Thread the liver and chicken pieces, alternately, on a bamboo stick (shaped into a needle) and keep aside for a few minutes.
- Heat the oil or ghee in a frying pan; lay the skewered bamboo sticks and cook covered till tender.
- Serve hot with any green salad.

CHICKEN SOUFFLÉ

PREPARATION TIME: 5 MIN.
COOKING TIME: 1 HR.
SERVES: 4

Ingredients

1 cup Chicken mince, cooked
2½ tbsp / 50 gm Butter
3 tbsp / 30 gm Refined flour (*maida*)
1 cup / 200 ml Milk
3 Egg yolks, beaten
Salt and black pepper (*kali mirch*) to taste
4 Egg whites

Method

- Melt the butter in a saucepan; add the flour and sauté for a minute. Remove from heat, and gradually mix in the milk. Return the pan to the heat and cook the sauce till it thickens, stirring constantly to prevent lumps from forming.
- Remove the pan from the heat and allow the sauce to cool a little. Then add the egg yolks, seasoning, and chicken.
- Whip the egg whites until stiff, and fold carefully into the chicken mixture.
- Transfer the mixture into a greased soufflé dish and bake in a moderately hot oven (180°C / 350°F) for about 30-40 minutes. The soufflé should be well risen when ready.
- Serve immediately.

Note: *This can also be made with minced ham, fish or sweetcorn.*

BAKED CHICKEN

PREPARATION TIME: 5 MIN.
COOKING TIME: 1 HR.
SERVES: 3

Ingredients

1 kg Chicken, broiler , whole
5 tbsp / 100 gm Butter
1 cup / 200 ml Water
¼ cup / 50 ml Vinegar (*sirka*)
½ cup / 100 ml Tomato sauce
a dash Tabasco sauce
Salt to taste

Method

- ▹ Clean the chicken thoroughly; apply butter, taking care to put some inside the cavity.
- ▹ Mix the remaining ingredients together. Pour the mixture over the chicken in a baking dish and bake in a moderately hot oven (180°C / 350°C) for one hour or till the chicken is brown and succulent.
- ▹ Serve hot.

TIME BOUND

POULTRY COOKS AND TASTES BEST IF USED WITHIN 8-24 HOURS AFTER SLAUGHTER.

BAKED CHICKEN WITH CREAM CHEESE

PREPARATION TIME: 5 MIN.
COOKING TIME: 30 MIN.
SERVES: 4

Ingredients

1 kg Chicken, broiler
½ cup / 100 gm Cream cheese (hang 3 cups yoghurt in a muslin cloth till all the water drains out)
¾ cup / 150 ml Cream, whipped
1 tsp / 2 gm Mustard powder
½ tbsp / 9 gm Ginger (*adrak*) paste
2-3 tbsp / 30-45 ml Worcestershire sauce
Salt and black pepper (*kali mirch*) to taste

Method

- Mix all the ingredients together (except the chicken) in a bowl.
- Place the chicken in an ovenproof dish and pour the sauce over it.
- Bake in a moderately hot oven (180°C / 350°F) for 30 minutes or till the chicken is tender and browned. There should be some gravy left.
- Serve hot.

ROAST CHICKEN WITH LEMON JUICE AND ROSEMARY

PREPARATION TIME: 2 HRS.
COOKING TIME: 1 HR.
SERVES: 3

Ingredients

1 kg Chicken, whole
½-¾ cup / 100-150 ml Lemon (*nimbu*) juice
4 Garlic (*lasan*) cloves, unpeeled
a few strips Bacon, cut lengthwise
a few sprigs Rosemary
Salt and black pepper (*kali mirch*) to taste
1 cup / 200 ml Chicken stock (see p. 9)

Method

- Pour two tbsp lemon juice and sprinkle a little salt in the chicken cavity. Add the garlic cloves.
- Rub the chicken with a little salt and some olive oil to keep it moist.
- Pour the remaining lemon juice over the chicken. Put strips of bacon fat or any other fat on the chicken breasts.
- Add rosemary and marinate for two hours.
- Pour the chicken stock, 3 tbsp lemon juice, (if less, squeeze another lemon and add the rind as well), a sprig of rosemary, and the remaining garlic. Cover and bake in a moderately hot oven (180°C / 350°F) for 45 minutes or till the chicken is tender. Remove the cover in the last 15 minutes of roasting so that the chicken may brown.
- Slice the breast portion first into thin pieces and then the rest of the chicken. Pour the gravy over it.
- Serve with roasted potatoes and onions and some green vegetables.

CASSEROLE CHICKEN WITH VEGETABLES

PREPARATION TIME: 10 MIN.
COOKING TIME: 2½ HRS.
SERVES: 4

Ingredients

1 kg Chicken, skinned, cut into pieces
2 tbsp / 40 gm Unsalted butter
Salt and black pepper (*kali mirch*) to taste
1 tsp / 3 gm Sugar
1 tbsp / 4 gm Green coriander (*hara dhaniya*) / Parsley, finely chopped
1 tsp Mint (*pudina*) leaves, chopped
2-3 Onions, large, cut into rings
200 gm Mushrooms, fresh, sliced
500 gm Spinach (*palak*), finely chopped
250 gm Potatoes, peeled, thickly sliced
2 cups / 400 ml Chicken stock (see p. 9)
½ cup / 100 ml Cream

Method

- Melt the unsalted butter over medium heat in a large pan. Sauté the chicken pieces until golden brown. Remove and arrange them in a deep casserole.
- Mix the salt, pepper, sugar, and the herbs together, and sprinkle some over the chicken. Layer half the onions, mushrooms, spinach, and potatoes on top of the chicken, sprinkling a little of the herb mixture. Repeat in the same order.
- Cover the casserole and bake in a preheated oven (180°C / 350°F) for about two hours. Remove the casserole cover in the last 15-20 minutes to brown. Serve hot.

CHICKEN WITH COTTAGE CHEESE & PINEAPPLE

PREPARATION TIME: 1½ HRS.
COOKING TIME: 40 MIN.
SERVES: 4

Ingredients

8 Chicken breasts

For the marinade
1 tbsp / 18 gm Garlic (*lasan*) paste
1 tbsp / 18 gm Ginger (*adrak*) paste
2 tbsp / 30 ml Lemon (*nimbu*) juice
Salt to taste
Red chilli powder to taste

For the filling
250 gm Cottage cheese (*paneer*), mashed
3 Pineapple rings, finely chopped
Salt and white pepper (*safed mirch*) to taste
2 Green chillies, deseeded, finely chopped

For the batter
2 Eggs
1 tbsp / 10 gm Cornflour
3 tbsp / 30 gm Refined flour (*maida*)
Salt to taste
Ghee or refined oil for deep-frying

Method

- Clean the chicken breasts and debone, keeping the winglet bone intact. With a sharp knife, cut open the breast piece starting from the thick edge of the breast, taking care not to separate it, open the flap and flatten the piece.
- For the marinade, mix all the ingredients together and rub over the breast on the flattened side. Marinate for one hour.

- For the filling, mix all the ingredients together. Divide the filling into eight portions, and stuff each portion in the centre of the marinated chicken breasts and fold to make a round ball, with the bone sticking out. Refrigerate for 30 minutes.
- For the batter, mix the ingredients with ½ cup water. Dip the stuffed breasts in the batter and deep-fry till golden brown.
- To re-heat the fried chicken breasts grease a roasting tray. Arrange the pieces on it and roast in a preheated oven (190°C / 375°F) for about 15 minutes.
- Serve immediately with salad or green vegetables.

FOR TENDER CHICKEN

THE LONGER YOU MARINATE CHICKEN, MINIMUM 8-10 HOURS, THE MORE TENDER IT WILL BE.

CHICKEN IN ORANGE SAUCE

PREPARATION TIME: 10 MIN.
COOKING TIME: 10-15 MIN.
SERVES: 4

Ingredients

3 cups Chicken, cooked, cubed
3 tbsp / 60 gm Sugar
3 tbsp / 45 ml Malt vinegar (*sirka*)
1 tsp / 2 gm Cornflour, dissolved in 2 tbsp water
3 Oranges, small, segmented with the membranes removed

Method

- Cook the sugar and vinegar in a pan till the sugar caramelizes to light brown. Add the cornflour paste. Cook till the syrup thickens.
- Add the orange segments and chicken. Mix thoroughly.
- Remove from heat and serve immediately.

CHICKEN ROAST IN YOGHURT WITH VEGETABLES

PREPARATION TIME: 6-8 HRS.
COOKING TIME: 30-40 MIN.
SERVES: 4

Ingredients

1 kg Chicken, broiler
1 tsp / 6 gm Ginger-garlic (*adrak-lasan*) paste
½ cup / 100 gm Yoghurt (*dahi*)
Salt to taste
1 tbsp / 15 ml Vinegar (*sirka*)
3-4 tsp / 15-20 gm Butter
4-5 Onions, small, finely chopped
1 Capsicum (*Shimla mirch*), large, sliced
4-5 Onions, small, cross-cut in the centre
100 gm Mushrooms, halved

Method

- Marinate the chicken in ginger-garlic paste, yoghurt and salt for 6-8 hours, covered, in a refrigerator.
- Cook the chicken in a pan with the marinade. Add vinegar and brown slowly. Cook till tender.
- Heat the butter in another pan; sauté the onions till brown. Add the chicken, sprinkle some water and keep stirring so that it gets evenly browned.
- Add the remaining ingredients and 2 tsp butter; stir-fry on high heat till the mixture is dry.
- Serve hot with mashed potatoes.

CHICKEN IN WHITE SAUCE–INDIAN STYLE

PREPARATION TIME: 5-8 MIN.
COOKING TIME: 20 MIN.
SERVES: 4

Ingredients

1 kg Chicken, cut into pieces
2 Onions, medium-sized, sliced
1 Ginger (*adrak*), chopped, 1″ piece
4-6 Garlic (*lasan*) cloves, chopped
8 Black peppercorns (*sabut kali mirch*)
3½ tbsp / 70 gm Butter
3 tbsp / 30 gm Refined flour (*maida*)
1 cup / 200 ml Milk
1 cup / 200 ml Chicken stock (see p. 9)
1-2 Tomatoes, large, chopped
2 Green chillies, slit, deseeded
a pinch, Kashmiri chilli powder

Method

- Boil the chicken with one onion, ginger, garlic, and black peppercorns. Remove and cut into pieces.
- Heat three tbsp butter in a pan; sauté the remaining onions till transparent. Add flour and sauté till cooked but not browned. Remove from heat. Gradually add milk and chicken stock, stirring constantly. Add the cooked chicken. Cook on low heat till the sauce thickens.
- Heat the remaining butter in a separate pan; sauté the tomatoes till soft. Add green chillies and chilli powder, remove from heat and add to the sauce.

CHICKEN STROGANOFF

PREPARATION TIME: 5 MIN.
COOKING TIME: 40 MIN.
SERVES: 4

Ingredients

1 kg Chicken, cut into pieces
Salt to taste
1 Onion, medium-sized
10 Black peppercorns (*sabut kali mirch*)
200 gm Mushrooms, halved
4 tsp / 8 gm Cornflour, dissolved in 3 tbsp water
1-2 tbsp / 15-30 ml Vinegar (*sirka*)
2 tsp / 10 ml Soya sauce
1-2 tbsp / 15-30 ml Worcestershire sauce
2 tsp / 10 ml Lemon (*nimbu*) juice
½ cup / 100 ml Milk
1 Egg yolk (optional), well beaten
a little Cream

Method

- Boil the chicken in 3½ cups water. Add salt, onion, and black peppercorns. Debone the chicken and cut into cubes or strips. Keep the stock aside.
- Cook the mushrooms for a few minutes in one cup chicken stock. Heat the remaining stock. Add cornflour paste and cook till it thickens.
- Add the mushroom, chicken, vinegar, the sauces, and lemon juice; cook till the sauce thickens again. Add milk and mix. Add egg yolk, if using, and cream just before serving. Serve with steamed rice and salad.

POACHED CHICKEN WITH GINGER AND ORANGE

PREPARATION TIME: 10 MIN. – OVERNIGHT
COOKING TIME: 1½ HRS.
SERVES: 4

Ingredients

1½ kg Roasting chicken,with skin
1 Ginger (*adrak*), 1″ piece
3 Carrots (*gajar*), peeled, chopped
1 Onion, chopped
3 Orange zest, long strips, pith removed
2 Parsley stalks
4-6 Black peppercorns (*sabut kali mirch*)
1¼ cups / 250 ml White wine
1½ tbsp / 30 gm Butter
2 tsp / 4 gm Cornflour
6 tbsp / 120 ml Double cream
½ tsp / 1 gm Black pepper (*kali mirch*), freshly ground
Salt to taste

Method

- Remove fat from the chicken cavity, wash and wipe inside out.
- Peel ⅓ of the ginger and slice into thin rounds. Carefully loosen the skin from the chicken breasts and legs; push the ginger slices beneath the skin. Truss the chicken with a white string. Place it in a heavy, deep, ovenproof dish, and add half of the remaining ginger, peeled and chopped; carrots, onion, two strips orange zest, parsley, black peppercorns and wine.
- Pour in water to come half way round the chicken. Cover the dish and keep overnight in the refrigerator for the flavours to mingle.

- ▹ The next day bring the dish to room temperature and then cook. Skim thoroughly, add salt and cover the chicken breasts with a double thickness of washed and wrung out muslin, the ends of which should fall into the broth to draw this over the bird and baste it during cooking. Lower heat until the liquid simmers slowly, cover dish with a close-fitting lid and poach for one hour.
- ▹ Test chicken if done by pressing its flesh and seeing if you can move its legs, in their sockets. If in doubt, poach for a few minutes more.
- ▹ Carefully strain three cups stock. Keep the chicken hot in a slow oven.
- ▹ Let the fat rise to the top of the pan of stock as you heat the cream with cornflour in a small bowl. Decrease the stock, whisk some of this into the cream and cornflour to warm them, and whisk all together in a saucepan. Cook over low heat beating constantly until the sauce comes to the simmer. Add remaining ginger and orange zest to refresh the flavours, and let the sauce simmer very gently, whisking occasionally, for several minutes to reduce and thicken.
- ▹ When the sauce is ready, it should coat the back of a spoon. Season and strain into a heated boat. Drain, de-truss. Remove the ginger from under the chicken skin and serve with boiled vegetables.

ADVANCE DRESSING

CHICKEN SHOULD BE DRESSED AT LEAST 10-12 HOURS BEFORE COOKING. THE MEAT WHEN COOKED, TASTES NICE AND SOFT AND DOES NOT HAVE ANY TOUGH LEATHERY TASTE.

NO-FUSS CHICKEN WITH MUSHROOMS

PREPARATION TIME: 15 MIN.
COOKING TIME: 40 MIN.
SERVES: 4

Ingredients

2 Chickens (1 kg each), broilers, cut into 8 pieces
Salt and black pepper (*kali mirch*) to taste
1 ⅔ / 250 gm Butter
4 tbsp / 40 gm Refined flour (*maida*)
2 cups / 400 ml Chicken stock (see p. 9)
3 tsp / 6 gm Mustard powder
½ cup / 100 ml Tomato sauce
4 tsp / 20 ml Worcestershire sauce
Kashmiri chilli powder or paprika to taste
200 gm Mushrooms,

Method

- Marinate the chicken with salt and black pepper for 15 minutes.
- Melt the butter in a heavy-bottomed pan; add the chicken and brown on high heat. Remove the chicken from the pan. In the same pan, add flour and stir till well blended. Add chicken stock and cook until the mixture thickens, stirring constantly.
- Mix mustard powder, the two sauces, and chilli powder together. Add this to the above sauce.
- Add the mushrooms and fried chicken pieces; cook covered on low heat till the chicken is tender.
- Serve hot with hot potato salad (see p. 138).

CHICKEN CHASSEUR

PREPARATION TIME: 30 MIN.
COOKING TIME: 2 HRS.
SERVES: 4

Ingredients

1 kg Chicken, broiler, cut into 4 pieces
6½ tbsp / 65 gm Refined flour (*maida*)
1 ¾cup / 75 gm Butter
2 Onions, sliced
100 gm Mushrooms, chopped
250 gm Tomatoes, skinned, chopped
100 gm Bacon, fried (optional)
150-200 gm Sausages (optional)

For the sauce
2 cups / 400 ml Chicken stock (see p. 9)
3 tbsp / 45 ml Red wine
1 tsp / 2 gm Rosemary, dried, ground
2 sprigs Parsley
2 Bay leaf (*tej patta*)
½ tsp / 1 gm Black peppercorns (*sabut kali mirch*), freshly ground
Salt to taste

Method

- Coat the chicken well with five tbsp flour, mixed with salt.
- Heat 2½ tbsp butter in a pan; fry the chicken till golden brown. Remove and put into a casserole.
- Heat the remaining butter in a pan; add the onions and sauté till soft. Add the mushrooms and tomatoes. Sauté for a few minutes. Put these in the casserole. (You can also add bacon or sausages or both.)
- For the sauce, make a paste of the remaining flour with a little water and add to the chicken stock along with the wine, rosemary, parsley, bay leaf, black pepper, and salt. Cook until the sauce thickens slightly and then pour over the chicken and vegetable mixture.
- Cover the casserole and cook in a moderately hot oven (180°C / 350°F) for 1½ hours or until done.

BOILED CHICKEN

PREPARATION TIME: 10-15 MIN.
COOKING TIME: 1-2½ HRS.
SERVES: 4-6

Ingredients

1 Boiling fowl
4 Onions, medium, peeled
4 Carrots (*gajar*), large, peeled, cut into large pieces
1 Lemon (*nimbu*), sliced
Salt and black pepper (*kali mirch*) to taste

For the sauce

1¾cup / 75 gm Butter
5 tbsp / 50 gm Refined flour (*maida*)
100 gm Mushrooms
1 cup / 200 ml Milk
2 cups / 400 ml Chicken stock (see p. 9)
a pinch Nutmeg (*jaiphal*), grated

Method

- Wash the fowl under running water and put into a pan or pressure cooker with the giblets, excluding the liver.
- Put the onions, carrots, lemon, and seasoning in enough water. Bring to the boil, lower heat and cook gently for about two hours in the pan or for half an hour in a pressure cooker. Remove the meat and strain.
- For the sauce, heat 1¾ tbsp butter in a small pan; sauté the mushrooms. Remove and keep aside.
- Heat the remaining butter in the pan; add the flour and sauté for several minutes. Gradually blend the milk and chicken stock and stir continuously so that there are no lumps. Cook till the sauce thickens. Add the mushrooms and nutmeg. Mix well.
- Put the chicken pieces on a serving platter with vegetables around it. Pour the white sauce over the chicken. Garnish with parsley, green coriander or mint.

Note: *The liver of the chicken is inclined to give the stock a slightly bitter taste.*

CHICKEN IN YOGHURT SAUCE

PREPARATION TIME: 10 MIN.
COOKING TIME: 30 MIN.
SERVES: 4

Ingredients

4-5 Chicken breasts, skinned
¾ cup / 150 gm Yoghurt (*dahi*), thick
1 Onion, large, chopped
6 Garlic (*lasan*) cloves, chopped
2 Green chillies, deseeded
1 tsp / 1½ gm Coriander (*dhaniya*) powder
3 tbsp / 45 gm Ghee
1″ stick Cinnamon (*dalchini*)
5 Green cardamoms (*choti elaichi*)
10 Cloves (*laung*)
1 tsp / 6 gm Ginger (*adrak*), ground
1 tsp / 4 gm Salt
1 tsp / 2 gm Black pepper (*kali mirch*)

Method

- Make three deep cuts on each breast with a sharp knife.
- Blend yoghurt, onion, garlic, green chillies and coriander powder; mix with the chicken. Marinate covered, overnight, in the refrigerator.
- Drain the chicken, reserving the marinade. Melt ghee in an ovenproof casserole; fry the chicken for 10 minutes until evenly browned. Add spices, seasoning, and reserved marinade; mix well.
- Cover the casserole and bake (at 190°C / 375°F) until tender and some sauce remains. Serve hot.

CHICKEN BREASTS IN RED WINE

PREPARATION TIME: 5 MIN.
COOKING TIME: 2 HRS.
SERVES: 4

Ingeredients

4 Chicken breasts, boned
6¼ tbsp / 125 gm Unsalted butter
1 Onion, large, finely chopped
½ cup / 100 ml Red wine
½ cup / 100 ml Chicken stock (see p. 9)
Salt and black pepper (*kali mirch*) to taste

Method

- Heat 2½ tbsp butter in a pan; add the chicken and cook over gentle heat for 20 minutes or until tender. Remove and arrange the chicken on a serving dish.
- Add the onion to the pan with the wine; bring to the boil and continue to boil for one minute. Add the chicken stock and boil briskly until the mixture is reduced to half.
- Stir in the remaining butter in small blobs, and season to taste.
- Just before serving pour the sauce over the chicken.

ROAST CHICKEN WITH ORANGE SAUCE

PREPARATION TIME: 10 MIN.
COOKING TIME: 2 HRS.
SERVES: 4-6

Ingredients

2 Chickens, broiler (1 kg each)
2 Oranges, small, peeled
Salt and black pepper (*kali mirch*) to taste
4 tbsp / 60 gm Marmalade or orange jam

For the sauce

1¼ tbsp / 25 gm Butter
1 Carrot (*gajar*), peeled, finely chopped
1 Onion, peeled, finely chopped
1 Celery, chopped
2 cups / 400 ml Chicken stock (see p. 8)
2½ tbsp / 25 gm Refined flour (*maida*)
Grated rind and juice of 1 orange
Salt and black pepper (*kali mirch*) to taste

Method

- Put the oranges into the carcasses of the chickens. Keep the birds in a roasting tin and season with salt and pepper. Roast in a moderately hot oven (180°C/ 350°F) for about half an hour.
- Smear the surface with jam, then return the chicken to the oven and continue to roast for another hour, basting it continuously with the marmalade or orange jam. Do not allow it to brown too quickly. Can also be roasted in a covered pan.
- For the sauce, melt the butter in a heavy skillet; add the refined flour and sauté gently. Add all the vegetables and sauté until golden. Add the stock, bring the sauce to the boil and simmer for 20 minutes.
- Add the orange rind and juice. Season with salt and pepper.
- Take the chicken out of the pan and serve it on a hot dish. Remove the fat from the roasting tin and pour the sediment into the sauce. Reheat and pour the sauce over the chicken or serve it separately.

PERFECT FRIED CHICKEN

PREPARATION TIME: 10 MIN.
COOKING TIME: 40-50 MIN.
SERVES: 4

Ingredients

2 Chickens, broilers, halved (750 gm each)
1¼ cup / 25 gm Refined flour (*maida*)
Salt, pepper and paprika to taste
Refined oil for frying

Method

- Combine flour and seasonings in a paper or plastic bag. Chop the chicken into medium sized pieces. Add two or three pieces at a time and shake. Place on a rack to allow the coating to dry.
- Heat the oil in a heavy-bottomed pan; add the chicken, a few pieces a time, for about 15-20 minutes or till it browns, taking care not to break the pieces when turning them round. When lightly browned, reduce heat and cover the pan tightly. If the cover is not tight, add a little hot water. Cook for 10-20 minutes or until tender.
- Uncover the last 10 minutes to make the chicken crisp. Remove and repeat till all are fried.

LAMB

LAMB ROAST

PREPARATION TIME: 2 HRS.
COOKING TIME: 1 HR.
SERVES: 4

Ingredients

1 kg Leg of lamb
1-1½ tsp / 4-6 gm Salt
½ cup / 100 gm Yoghurt (*dahi*)
or
2-3 tbsp / 30-45 ml Malt vinegar (*sirka*)
8-12 Garlic (*lasan*) cloves, ground
1 Ginger (*adrak*), ground, ½″ piece
2 tbsp / 30 ml Refined oil
2 Black cardamoms (*badi elaichi*)
½ Onion, sliced

Method

- With a large fork, pierce the meat on all sides, rub in the salt.
- Beat the yoghurt well, mix in the garlic and ginger pastes. Marinate the meat with this mixture and keep aside for two hours. If using vinegar, marinate as above.
- Heat the oil in a pressure cooker; add the lamb with the marinade, black cardamoms, and onion; sauté till the lamb is browned. Add enough water for it to cook in the pressure cooker for 20 minutes. Allow it to cool on its own.

- With an ordinary lid on the cooker, simmer the roast for another 15 minutes or until the lamb is tender and the liquid has dried up. Remove the lamb and keep aside. Strain the stock.
- In another pan, add a little flour and sauté till brown. Add one cup lamb stock and cook on low heat till slightly thick.
- Cut the roast into slices. Cut against the grain and on a slant. Arrange them on a dish, pour some gravy over it and serve the rest of the gravy separately with roast potatoes.

Roast potatoes: Peel and parboil the potatoes for 15 minutes. Before the lamb roast is ready add the potatoes and let them cook with the roast. The potatoes should preferably be medium-sized and cut in half lengthwise.

ALL ABOUT MEAT

MEAT IS AN IMPORTANT PROTEIN FOOD AND THE MOST EXPENSIVE TOO. THE BEST CUTS ARE USUALLY USED FOR ROASTING WHILE THE CHEAPER CUTS FOR STEWING OR SLOW COOKING.

SPICY LAMB ROLL

PREPARATION TIME: 2 HRS.
COOKING TIME: 15 MIN.
SERVES: 4

Ingredients

1 kg tender leg of lamb, cleaned, deboned and washed
2 Onions, large
a few Mint (*pudina*) leaves
a few Green chillies
Salt to taste
½ cup / 100 gm Yoghurt (*dahi*), mixed with ½ cup cream
12 Black peppercorns (*sabut kali mirch*)
2 Bay leaves (*tej patta*)
2 1″ sticks Cinnamon (*dalchini*)
6 Green cardamoms (*choti elaichi*)
½″ piece Ginger (*adrak*), ground
8 Garlic (*lasan*) cloves
Red chilli powder to taste (optional)
3 tbsp / 45 ml Refined oil

Method

- Spread out the meat and pound it gently. Grind one onion, mint leaves and green chillies with salt. Rub this paste well on one side of the lamb, make slight gashes so that the mixture seeps into the meat.
- Roll and tie the meat with thread. Pour yoghurt and cream mixture over lamb and coat it well. Let the lamb marinate for a couple of hours.
- Place the rolls in a heavy-bottomed pan, add one finely sliced onion and the whole spices, ginger, garlic, a little salt, and red chilli powder (optional). Mix well.
- Pour hot ghee and about 3-4 cups boiling water. Cover and simmer on low heat till the water is absorbed and the lamb is tender.
- Slice the lamb into thin slices. Arrange the slices on a platter overlapping each other in the centre. On either side put some boiled green peas with a dash of butter. Serve hot with a good salad and bread rolls.

MASALA RAAN

PREPARATION TIME: 2 HRS.
COOKING TIME: 3¼ HRS.
SERVES: 6

Ingredients

1½ kg Leg of lamb, washed

For the marinade
1½ cups / 300 gm Yoghurt (*dahi*)
1 tsp / 6 gm Ginger (*adrak*), ground
1 tsp / 6 gm Garlic (*lasan*), ground
Salt to taste
3 Green chillies

2 tbsp / 30 ml Refined oil
2-3 Onions, medium-sized, finely sliced
2-3 Tomatoes, medium-sized, grated
1 tbsp / 20 gm Poppy seeds (*khuskhus*), ground to a paste
½ tsp / 2½ gm Onion seeds (*chironji*)
1 tbsp / 4 gm Green coriander (*hara dhuniya*), chopped

Method

- For the marinade, mix all the ingredients and rub into the lamb. Keep aside for a few hours.
- Heat the oil in a wok (*kadhai*); add the onions and sauté till brown. Add the tomatoes, and stir-fry till the oil separates. Add the poppy seed paste, onion seeds, lamb along with the marinade and green coriander. Lower heat and let the lamb cook in its own juices for about three hours or until tender. Serve with naan.

QUICK DISH OF SAUSAGES

PREPARATION TIME: 5 MIN.
COOKING TIME: 30 MIN.
SERVES: 4

Ingredients

500 gm Sausages
4 Tomatoes, large
Salt and black pepper (*kali mirch*) to taste
1 tbsp / 15 ml Worcestershire sauce
500 gm Potatoes, boiled, mashed
1 tbsp / 20 gm Butter

Method

- Skin the tomatoes and sausages, and arrange them in alternate layers in a well-greased ovenproof dish.
- Sprinkle some salt, black pepper, and Worcestershire sauce; cover with mashed potatoes, adding more salt, black pepper and a little cream. Dot with butter and bake in the centre of the oven (at 150°C / 300°F) for 15-20 minutes or until golden brown.

MEAT MOULD

PREPARATION TIME: 10 MIN.
COOKING TIME: 1 HR.
SERVES: 4

Ingredients

500 gm Lamb, minced, cooked
1 cup / 120 gm Breadcrumbs
1 Onion, large, chopped
250 gm Potatoes, boiled, mashed
a bunch Green coriander (*hara dhaniya*), chopped
Salt and black pepper (*kali mirch*) to taste
1 tbsp / 15 ml Tomato sauce
1 Egg, beaten

Method

- Grease a mould or a cake tin thoroughly and coat it with golden crumbs.
- Mix the mince with the onion, potatoes, green coriander and seasoning. Bind with tomato sauce and egg and place in the mould or cake tin. Cover with crumbs and greased paper. Bake at 150°C / 300°F for an hour or until firm to the touch.
- Serve cold with salad.

BONELESS LAMB STEW WITH POTATO DUMPLINGS

PREPARATION TIME: 10 MIN.
COOKING TIME: 1 HR.
SERVES: 4

Ingredients

400 gm Lamb, boneless
1 tbsp / 10 gm Refined flour (*maida*)
Salt to taste
2 tbsp / 30 ml Refined oil
2 cups / 400 ml Stock (see p. 9)
1 Onion, large, peeled, diced
2 Carrots (*gajar*), large, peeled, diced
2 Celery, chopped

For the dumplings
250 gm Potatoes
1 Egg
1 Onion, small, peeled, minced
7½ tbsp / 75 gm Refined flour (*maida*) with 1 tsp baking powder
Salt and black pepper (*kali mirch*) to taste

Method

- Put the lamb and the seasoned flour in a paper bag and shake well, to coat the lamb completely.
- Heat the oil in a wok (*kadhai*); add the lamb and sauté on medium heat for a couple of minutes. Add the remaining flour from the paperbag. Stir, add stock and cook on low heat for 30 minutes or till lamb is tender, and cooked.
- In a separate pan, add all the vegetables with some water and a pinch of salt. Parboil and add these along with the water to the lamb mixture.
- For the dumplings, mix all the ingredients together and divide the mixture equally. Shape each portion into small balls, using a little flour to prevent sticking. Add the dumplings to the lamb mixture and cook. Cover and simmer for 30 minutes. Serve hot.

ECONOMICAL HAMBURGERS

PREPARATION TIME: 15 MIN.
COOKING TIME: 30 MIN.
SERVES: 12

Ingredients

1 kg Lamb, minced
3 Onions, large, finely diced
2 tsp / 8 gm Salt
Black pepper (*kali mirch*) to taste
1 cup / 120 gm White breadcrumbs
2 Eggs, beaten
6 tbsp / 90 ml Milk
1 cup / 100 gm Refined flour (*maida*), seasoned with salt and pepper
Refined oil for shallow frying
12 buns
3 tomatoes, sliced
Mustard paste, to taste
Mayonnaise, to taste
Butter, to taste

Method

- Mix all the ingredients well together except the oil.
- Divide the mixture equally into 12 balls. Flatten each portion into thin rounds.
- Heat the oil in a wok (*kadhai*); fry the rounds, a few at a time, till golden brown. The rounds will shrink and thicken during frying. Remove with a slotted spoon and drain the excess oil on paper towels.
- Cut the buns in half, toast one side, apply mayonnaise and butter mixture on the other side. Keep a lamb patty, some onion rings on the patty, and a slice of tomato and cover with the toasted half. If desired, use a little mustard paste.

LEFTOVER COLD MEAT

PREPARATION TIME: 10 MIN.
COOKING TIME: 20-30 MIN.
SERVES: 2

Ingredients

100 gm Minced cold lamb
1 tbsp / 15 gm Breadcrumbs, fine
¼ cup / 50 ml Milk, hot
Salt and black pepper (*kali mirch*) to taste
1 Lemon (*nimbu*) rind, grated
a pinch Oregano, dried
a pinch, Thyme, dried
2 Eggs, separated

Method

- ▹ Soak the breadcrumbs in milk, when they swell up, add the minced meat, seasoning, lemon rind, and dried herbs.
- ▹ Beat the egg yolks and mix with the lamb mixture. Beat the whites till stiff and fold in lightly. Transfer contents into a well-buttered pie dish and bake in a moderately hot oven (180°C / 350°F) for 20-30 minutes.

FRESH AND EASY

GARLIC STORED IN THE REFRIGERATOR REMAINS FRESH AND IS EASIER TO PEEL.

LAMB STEAK

PREPARATION TIME: 10 MIN.
COOKING TIME: 30-40 MIN.
SERVES: 6

Ingredients

1½ kg Leg of lamb, deboned
Salt to taste
2 tbsp / 30 ml Refined oil
1½ Onions, large, minced
1″ piece Ginger (*adrak*), ground
12 Garlic (*lasan*) cloves, ground
2 Black cardamoms (*badi elaichi*)
5 Cloves (*laung*)
1″ stick Cinnamon (*dalchini*)

Method

- Cut the meat into flat steak pieces, cut across the grain. Prick each piece with a fork and rub it with salt. Let the lamb stand for 3-4 hours to tenderize.
- Heat the oil in a pan; add the onions and sauté for a few minutes. Add the ginger and garlic pastes and fry for a minute. Then add the lamb and cook over low heat for about 5-10 minutes. Close the pan with a fitting lid, cook on low heat and simmer till done. When the lamb is half cooked, add the black cardamoms, cloves and cinnamon stick for flavour. No water should be added.
- Serve hot garnished with lightly fried onion rings and tomatoes.

CUTLETS IN TOMATO GRAVY

PREPARATION TIME: 2 HRS.
COOKING TIME: 30-45 MIN.
SERVES: 6

Ingredients

1 kg Lamb, minced
2 Green chillies
1 Ginger (*adrak*), 1″ piece
6 Garlic (*lasan*) cloves
1 bunch Green coriander (*hara dhaniya*)
1 sprig Mint (*pudina*) leaves
2 Potatoes, boiled, mashed
2 Eggs, beaten
½ cup / 60 gm Breadcrumbs
Refined oil for deep-frying

For the tomato gravy

2 kg Tomatoes, ripe, red
2 Green chillies
1 Onion, chopped
4 Garlic (*lasan*) cloves
1 Dry red chilli
4 tbsp / 80 gm Sugar or half sugar and half jaggery

Grind to a smooth paste

2 tbsp / 8 gm Coconut (*nariyal*), grated
2 Dry red chillies
5 Almonds (*badam*)
½ tsp / 1 gm Coriander (*dhaniya*) seeds
½ tsp / 1 gm Cumin (*jeera*) seeds
½ tsp / 1 gm Poppy (*khuskhus*) seeds
1 tbsp / 15 gm Ghee

Method

- Grind the green chillies, ginger, garlic, green coriander, and mint to a smooth paste.
- Mix the paste with the mince and mashed potatoes. Divide the mixture equally into lemon-sized portions and shape each into cutlets. Dip the

cutlets in egg then coat with breadcrumbs and keep aside for a couple of hours in the refrigerator.

- Heat the oil in a wok (*kadhai*); lower the cutlets, a few at a time, and deep-fry till golden brown. Remove with a slotted spoon and drain the excess oil on paper towels. Repeat till all the cutlets are fried.
- For the tomato gravy, boil all the ingredients together with one cup of water. When the tomatoes turn soft remove, mash, sieve and keep aside to cool.
- Heat the ghee in a wok (*kadhai*); add the ground paste and sauté for a few minutes. Add the tomato mixture and simmer. If the mixture is too thick add some hot water. Cook till the rawness of the spices goes. Then add the sugar. Arrange the cutlets in a dish and pour the gravy over it. Serve hot.

POUND OF FLESH!

IF THE MEAT IS BONELESS, BUY 100-125 GM PER SERVING. IF IT HAS A LITTLE BONE, ALLOW 175-225 GM PER SERVING. FOR CUTS WITH A HIGH PROPORTION OF BONE, YOU MAY NEED AS MUCH AS 350 GM PER SERVING.

STUFFED SHOULDER OF LAMB

PREPARATION TIME: 10 MIN.
COOKING TIME: 40 MIN.
SERVES: 4

Ingredients

1 kg Shoulder of lamb, deboned
Salt and black pepper (*kali mirch*) to taste

For the filling
250 gm Lamb, minced
2 large slices of Bread, soaked in water for 1 minute
2 Eggs, hard-boiled, cut into slices
1 Egg, raw
1 Onion, minced
1 tbsp / 4 gm Green coriander (*hara dhaniya*), chopped
2 Green chillies, deseeded, minced

Method

- Pound the lamb shoulder well and rub with salt and black pepper.
- For the filling, squeeze out the slices of bread from the water and add to the mince. Add the remaining ingredients and mix well.
- Stuff the filling into the lamb shoulder. Stitch it up.
- Roast either in the oven or cook in a pressure cooker. When tender, slice slantwise and serve with green peas and new potatoes in mint.

BAKED KEBABS

PREPARATION TIME: 10 MIN.
COOKING TIME: 40 MIN.
SERVES: 6

Ingredients

750 gm Lamb, minced
½ tsp / 1 gm Red chilli powder
½ tsp Mixed spices, ground (1 stick cinnamon, 2 cloves, 3 green cardamoms, 1 black cardamom, 1 glade mace and a pinch of nutmeg)
1 Onion, large, chopped
1″ piece Ginger (*adrak*)
10 Garlic (*lasan*) cloves, ground
1½ Bread, slices, soaked in ¼ cup milk
2 Green chillies, deseeded, chopped
½ tsp / 1 gm Coriander (*dhaniya*) seeds, roasted, ground
½ tsp / 1 gm Green coriander (*hara dhaniya*), chopped
1 Egg
6 tbsp / 60 gm Seasoned flour
Refined oil for shallow frying
Salt to taste
½ cup / 100 ml Cream
¼ cup / 50 gm Yoghurt (*dahi*), thick

Method

- Combine the mince with the first 11 ingredients. Mix well with hand and shape into 12 flat rounds about ½″ thick and 2″ in diameter. Roll lightly in flour and shallow fry in very little oil till brown on all sides. Remove and drain the excess oil on paper towels.
- Arrange the kebabs side by side in a shallow glass baking dish. Mix cream and yoghurt and pour over the kebabs. Bake in a moderately hot oven (180°C / 350°F) for half an hour or till kebabs are tender.

LAMB STEAK – FRENCH STYLE

PREPARATION TIME: 30 MIN.
COOKING TIME: 30 MIN.
SERVES: 4

Ingredients

4 Lamb steaks, medium-sized
1″ piece Papaya, raw, peeled, ground
1 tbsp / 15 ml Lemon (*nimbu*) juice
1 tbsp / 15 ml Vinegar (*sirka*)
1 tbsp / 20 gm Butter
1 tbsp / 15 ml Refined oil
1 tsp / 5 gm Mustard paste
1-2 tbsp / 15-30 gm Wine (red or white)
3 tbsp / 60 ml Cream

Method

- Tenderize the lamb with papaya or lemon juice and vinegar for 30 minutes.
- Heat the butter and oil in a heavy-based pan; add the steak and cook till done and browned on both sides. Remove the steak from the pan and pour out the surplus oil.
- In the same pan, add mustard paste and pour a little wine after ½ minute. Pour three tbsp thick cream and mix well. Put the steak back and let it cook in this sauce. Keep hot.
- Serve hot with parboiled green beans, onions, potatoes sautéed in butter.

PEPPER LAMB CHOPS

PREPARATION TIME: 5 MIN.
COOKING TIME: 30 MIN.
SERVES: 4

Ingredients

8 Lamb chops
3 tbsp / 60 gm Butter and oil
1 Onion, medium-sized, sliced
1 tsp / 2 gm Black pepper (*kali mirch*), coarsely ground
1 tsp / 6 gm Ginger (*adrak*) paste
1 tsp / 6 gm Garlic (*lasan*) paste
½-1 cup / 100-200 ml Red wine
3-4 Onions, large, cut into rings
2 Tomatoes, large, sliced

Method

- Heat the butter and oil in a pan; add the onion and sauté for a while. Add black pepper, stir for a second and then add two to three chops at a time. Sauté till well browned.
- When the meat is done, add ginger and garlic pastes. Cook for a couple of minutes then add the red wine.
- Cook on low heat adding a little water, if necessary, till the chops are tender. Top with onion rings and tomatoes. Cook covered for two minutes more.

SPICY LAMB CHOPS

PREPARATION TIME: 30 MIN.
COOKING TIME: 30 MIN.
SERVES: 2

Ingredients

250 gm lamb chops, washed and pat dried
1 tbsp / 15 gm Vinegar (*sirka*)
Red chilli powder to taste (optional)
Salt to taste
2 sprigs Curry leaves (*kadhi patta*)
1 tsp / 1½ gm Cumin-coriander (*jeera-dhaniya*) powder
Refined oil for frying
2 sprigs Mint (*pudina*) leaves, finely chopped

Method

- Mix vinegar, red chilli powder, salt, cumin-coriander powder, and curry leaves together. Make a few slashes on both sides of the chops and marinate in the vinegar mixture for half an hour.
- Heat the oil in a heavy-bottomed pan; add the marinated chops with the marinade and cook covered till the moisture dries. Remove the cover and brown the chops. Add the mint leaves.
- Cook the chops further with a little water till tender. Serve with any desired garnishing for example; spring onions, tomatoes or capsicum.

Note: *This recipe can also be made using pork chops.*

SANDWICH BAKE

PREPARATION TIME: 30 MIN.
COOKING TIME: 30 MIN.
SERVES: 2

Ingredients

2-3 Slices of lamb roast, finely chopped
100 gm Cottage cheese (*paneer*)
1 tsp / 6 gm Onion, finely chopped
2 White bread slices, crusts removed
2 Brown bread slices
2 Eggs
Salt to taste
1½ cups / 300 ml Black pepper (*kali mirch*) to taste
Milk
Red chilli powder to taste (optional)
1 tbsp / 20 gm Butter

Method

- Mix the cottage cheese with the lamb, and onion. Spread this mixture over two slices of bread, top with the remaining two slices. Cut each sandwich into four, and arrange in an ovenproof dish.
- Whisk eggs, black pepper and salt; mix in the milk. Pour this over the sandwiches. Dot with butter and allow it to stand for half an hour.
- Stand the dish in a pan of water to half the depth of the dish. Cook in a slow oven (150°C / 300°F) for 30 minutes or until slightly set.
- Serve hot with green vegetables or salad.

Note: *This recipe can also be made with ham.*

WHITE OR IRISH STEW

PREPARATION TIME: 10 MIN.
COOKING TIME: 30-40 MIN.
SERVES: 4

Ingredients

500 gm Shoulder of lamb, cut into large pieces
1 tsp / 5 ml Refined oil
2 Black cardamoms (*badi elaichi*)
1″ stick Cinnamon (*dalchini*), broken into smaller pieces
4-6 Cloves (*laung*)
10 Black peppercorns (*sabut kali mirch*)
1 Onion, cut into 4 pieces
1 Potato, peeled, cut into 6 pieces
1″ piece Ginger (*adrak*), julienned
10 Potatoes, small, peeled
10 Onions, small, peeled
4 Carrots (*gajar*), peeled, cut into thick, long strips
1 Cauliflower (*phool gobi*), broken into flowerets
4 Green chillies, whole with stalks

For the white sauce

1 tsp / 5 ml Refined oil
2 tbsp / 20 gm Refined flour (*maida*)
2 cups / 400 ml Milk
1 tbsp / 20 ml Double cream, optional

Method

- Heat the oil in a pressure cooker; sauté the whole spices for a minute. Add the meat and sauté on high heat, so that the juices of the meat get sealed. If required, keep sprinkling water on the meat, so that it does not get burnt. Sauté for about five minutes.
- Add the onion, potato and ginger. Stir and mix for a minute. Add salt and enough hot water so that a gravy will be left, after the meat has been cooked.

- ▹ Pressure cook for 20 minutes, first on a high flame, then lower the flame, depending on the toughness of the meat. Let the steam go down on its own. Open the pressure cooker and check whether the meat is ¾ cooked. If so, add the potatoes and onions. After five minutes, add the carrots, cauliflower and whole green chillies and cook for five minutes more.
- ▹ Meanwhile, make the white sauce. Heat the oil in a pan; add the flour, when it starts bubbling, remove from heat and add warm milk, gradually, beating the mixture thoroughly, so that there are no lumps. Cook the sauce till it thickens, and add to the stew. Let the stew simmer for about 10 minutes, being careful that the vegetables are not overcooked.
- ▹ Add the beaten cream; mix well and remove the pan from the heat. When serving remove the green chillies and whole spices.
- ▹ Serve with garlic bread or rice.

HOT ENOUGH TO GRILL

TO GRILL MEAT, MAKE SURE THAT THE GRILL IS REALLY HOT BEFORE THE FOOD IS PUT UNDERNEATH. THIS IS IMPORTANT SINCE THE HEAT OF THE GRILL SEALS IN THE FLAVOUR OF THE MEAT AT ONCE.

Note: *This humble dish is very nourishing and easy to make, but a little time-consuming.*

INDIAN-STYLE GRILLED CHOPS

PREPARATION TIME: 5 MIN.
COOKING TIME: 40 MIN.
SERVES: 5

Ingredients

1 kg Lamb chops, tender
1 tsp / 6 gm Ginger (*adrak*), ground
1 tsp / 6 gm Garlic (*lasan*), ground
1 tbsp / 15 ml Lemon (*nimbu*) juice
4-5 tbsp / 60-75 ml Refined oil
½ tsp / 1 gm Cumin (*jeera*) seeds
8 Onions, large, cut into thin roundels
1 tsp / 3 gm Sugar
1-2 tbsp / 15-30 ml Malt vinegar (*sirka*)
Salt to taste

Method

- Marinate the chops in ginger and garlic pastes and lemon juice for two to three hours.
- Heat the oil in a wok (*kadhai*); add cumin seeds. When it gives off an aroma of its own, add half the onions and sauté till light brown. Add sugar, malt vinegar, marinated chops, and salt. Cook covered on low heat till the water dries. Cook for a couple of minutes. Then add two cups hot water, cover and cook till the chops are tender. Check and stir, from time to time. If required, add more hot water.
- Towards the last few minutes add the remaining onions and cook till a little sauce remains and till the meat is moist. Serve with mashed potatoes.

Note: *This can also be made with chicken breasts*

ITALIAN LAMB DISH

PREPARATION TIME: 15 MIN.
COOKING TIME: 40 MIN.
SERVES: 4

Ingredients

500 gm Lamb, boneless
2 tbsp / 30 ml Refined oil
500 gm Carrots (*gajar*), peeled, diced
2 Potatoes, washed, peeled, diced
2 Onions, washed, peeled, diced
Salt and black pepper (*kali mirch*) to taste
2 sprigs Rosemary
2 sprigs Parsley

For the sauce

2 Egg yolks
2 tbsp / 30 ml Lemon (*nimbu*) juice
a little White wine
Salt and black pepper to taste
500 gm French beans, tender, washed, stringed

Method

- Heat the oil in a wok (*kadhai*); add lamb and sauté till brown. Add hot water and cook covered on medium flame till lamb is almost cooked.
- Remove cover and add carrots, potatoes, onions, salt, black pepper, rosemary, and parsely. If required, add a little water, so that when the dish is ready there will be some gravy. Cook till the lamb and vegetables are tender, taking care that the vegetables are not overcooked.
- For the sauce, mix egg yolks, lemon juice, white wine, salt, and a little pepper. Slightly beat the mixture and add to the stew. Cook on low heat for a minute or two or till the gravy is slightly thickened. Transfer on to a serving dish.
- Parboil the beans in sufficient water, so that no liquid is leftover. Then sauté the beans in butter in a heavy skillet and place them around the stew in the serving dish. Serve hot.

Note: *You can also use one whole egg and substitute the wine with the chicken stock. This also tastes good.*

ROYAL LAMB

PREPARATION TIME: 10 MIN.
COOKING TIME: 2 HRS. PLUS 50 MIN.
SERVES: 6

Ingredients

1½ kg Shoulder of lamb, washed, wiped with a damp cloth, with the knuckle left intact as this prevents shrinkage
1½ tbsp / 25 ml Refined oil or fat
100 gm Button mushrooms
1½ tbsp / 15 gm Refined flour (*maida*)
½ cup / 100 ml Dry cider or malt vinegar (*sirka*)
1 tbsp / 15 ml Tomato purée
a pinch of Sugar
Salt and black pepper (*kali mirch*) to taste
500 gm Baby carrots (*gajar*), peeled
500 gm Potatoes, scrubbed
a few sprigs Mint (*pudina*) leaves

Method

- ▹ Melt the oil or fat in a large roasting tin; add the shoulder and brown the joint quickly on all sides. Remove and add the mushrooms. Sauté and then add the flour; mix well. Add the cider or malt vinegar, tomato purée, sugar, salt and black pepper.
- ▹ Cook over gentle heat until smooth and thick. Since a lot of moisture comes out of the meat and vegetables during cooking, the gravy will be thinner initially.

- Put the meat back into the roasting tin, sprinkle it with salt and pepper, lay the mint sprigs over it, and cover the tin tightly with an aluminium foil, tucking it in carefully round the edges. Cook in the oven, on the top shelf at 170°C / 325°F for 2½ hours. One can also cook in the pressure cooker, in which case, cook the joint until half done. Then add the remaining ingredients, and cook covered in an ordinary pan with a well-fitting lid
- Carve the roast and arrange on the dish surrounded with vegetables. Serve the gravy separately.

FRESH AND GREEN

USE GREEN LEAFY VEGETABLES AS SOON AS THEY ARE BOUGHT AS THEY TEND TO DECAY AND LOSE THEIR FRESHNESS IF KEPT FOR TOO LONG.

TWIN MEAT LOAVES

PREPARATION TIME: 10 MIN.
COOKING TIME: 1 HR.
SERVES: 8

Ingredients

1 kg Lamb, minced
¼ cup / 30 gm Onions, finely chopped
2 tbsp Celery, chopped
2 tsp / 8 gm Salt
½ tsp / 1 gm Mustard powder
2 tbsp / 30 ml Worcestershire sauce
4 Soft bread, slices, crust removed
½-1 cup / 100-200 ml Milk
2-3 Eggs
½ cup / 60 gm Breadcrumbs
1 cup / 200 ml Chilli sauce

Method

- Mix the minced lamb with the next five ingredients.
- Soak the bread in milk and add the eggs. Beat with a rotary beater and then mix with the lamb mixture.
- Divide the mixture into two loaves and roll in breadcrumbs. Place the loaves in a greased-shallow dish.
- Pour ½ cup boiling water around the loaves and spread ½ cup chilli sauce on each loaf.
- Bake uncovered at 130°C / 250°F for one hour.

HAM LOAF

PREPARATION TIME: 10 MIN.
COOKING TIME: 15 MIN.
SERVES: 4

Ingredients

4 Ham slices
2 Eggs, separated
Salt, pepper, mustard powder to taste
¾ cup / 75 gm Refined flour (*maida*)
½ tsp / 3 gm Baking powder
1 Capsicum (*Shimla mirch*), medium, chopped
7-10 Mint (*pudina*) leaves

Method

- Beat the egg whites till frothy.
- Mix the salt, pepper and mustard powder into the egg yolks. Stir in the flour mixed with baking powder.
- Now fold in the egg whites, and bake as for a sponge cake, in an oven heated to 180°C for 20 to 20 minutes.
- Make a mixture of seasoned sliced ham, capsicum and mint for filling. Cut the flat sponge horizontally into three and place them one on top of the other with the ham mixture in between. Keep hot by putting it in the oven wrapped in foil till ready to eat.

MINCED MEAT BALLS

PREPARATION TIME: 5 MIN.
COOKING TIME: 1 HRS.
SERVES: 6

Ingredients

500 gm Meat from leg of lamb, finely minced
1 Onion, large
1″ piece Ginger (*adrak*), minced
a pinch Cumin (*jeera*) seeds, roasted, ground
Salt and black pepper (*kali mirch*) to taste

Method

- Mix all the ingredients together. Divide the mixture equally into small portions and shape each into marble-sized balls.
- Heat a little water in a wok (*kadhai*); add the meat balls and let them cook till tender. Then heat some oil in another wok and fry the balls till light brown. Add some tomato sauce, chilli sauce, and black pepper.
- Serve with drinks or at cocktail parties.

They can also be served for dinner, with a tomato gravy on spaghetti or steamed rice by adding the following ingredients:

2 cups / 400 ml Tomato juice
½ cup Carrots (*gajar*), chopped
½ cup Celery, chopped
Salt and black pepper to taste
1 cup Green peas (*matar*), shelled, boiled

Method

- Cook the tomato juice on low heat for 10 minutes. Add some water, carrots, celery, salt, and black pepper. Cover and simmer for 30 minutes. Add the peas.
- If the gravy is too thin, dissolve ¼ tsp cornflour with a little water and add this paste to the gravy; cook till it thickens.

Note: *It is very important that the meat must be from the leg portion, otherwise it will not bind.*

HOT AND COLD BATH

TOMATO SKINS CAN BE REMOVED EASILY IF TOMATOES ARE DIPPED FIRST IN HOT WATER AND THEN IN COLD WATER.

FISH & SEAFOOD

BOILED FISH WITH EGG SAUCE

PREPARATION TIME: 10 MIN.
COOKING TIME: 45 MIN.
SERVES: 4

Ingredients

1 kg Fish, cut into steaks
2 cups / 400 ml Water
1 Carrot (*gajar*), sliced
1 Onion, sliced
2 Cloves (*laung*)
8 Black peppercorns (*sabut kali mirch*)
1½-2 tbsp / 22-30 ml Vinegar (*sirka*)
Salt to taste

For the egg sauce
2 cups / 400 ml Milk
1 Onion, sliced
a pinch Mace (*javitri*)
8 Black peppercorns (*sabut kali mirch*)
1 Bay leaf (*tej patta*)
1½ tbsp / 30 gm Butter
1½ tbsp / 15 gm Refined flour (*maida*)
Salt and black pepper (*kali mirch*) to taste
2 Eggs, hard-boiled, coarsely chopped
Parsley, chopped for garnishing

Method

- Prepare the water in which the fish is to be boiled by mixing in all the remaining ingredients. Once the water comes to the boil, simmer for about 15 minutes, with the lid on. Let the mixture cool a little and add the fish. Bring the mixture to a slow boil, then let it simmer for 20 minutes. Lift the fish out carefully and drain. Keep aside in a warm dish.

- For the sauce, boil the onion and spices with the milk to let the flavours infuse. Cover the pan and keep near a warm place for 20 minutes or until it is well flavoured. Strain.
- Melt the butter in a pan; remove the pan from the heat and add the flour; mix well. Blend in the milk mixture. Return the pan to the heat and stir continuously until the sauce comes to the boil. Boil for several minutes so that the flour cooks thoroughly and the sauce is of a creamy consistency. Season to taste and add the eggs; mix well. Pour this sauce over the fish and garnish with parsley.

SOMETHING SMELLS FISHY!

TO REMOVE THE FISH ODOUR FROM A FRYING PAN, SPRINKLE SALT OVER IT, ADD HOT WATER AND LET IT STAND FOR A WHILE BEFORE WASHING.

FRIED SOLE FILLETS

PREPARATION TIME: 1 HR.
COOKING TIME: 15 MIN.
SERVES: 4

Ingredients

8 Sole fillets,washed under running water, dried
1 tbsp / 15 ml Lemon (*nimbu*) juice
Salt and black pepper (*kali mirch*) to taste
1 tbsp / 10 gm Seasoned flour
2 Eggs
½ cup / 60 gm Breadcrumbs
Refined oil for deep-frying

Method

- Marinate the fish in lemon juice, salt, and black pepper for half an hour to one hour. Roll the fillets in seasoned flour, dip in egg, and finally coat with breadcrumbs.
- Heat the oil in a wok (*kadhai*); deep-fry the fillets till golden brown. Remove with a slotted spoon and drain the excess oil on paper towels.
- Serve immediately with French fries and green salad.

ROLLED FILLETS OF FISH IN TOMATO SAUCE

PREPARATION TIME: 15 MIN. PLUS OVERNIGHT
COOKING TIME: 30 MIN.
SERVES: 4

Ingredients

1 kg Fish, deboned, skinned, cut into thin steaks

For the stuffing

Refined oil for frying
250 gm Potatoes, cut into pieces
2 Bread, slices
1 Onions, large, chopped
2-3 Eggs, hard-boiled, chopped

For the tomato sauce

750 gm-1 kg Tomatoes, fresh
1 tsp / 5 ml Onion juice
1 tsp / 6 gm Ginger (*adrak*) paste
1 tsp / 6 gm Garlic (*lasan*) paste
Salt to taste
a pinch Sugar
2 tbsp / 40 ml Cream (optional)

Method

- For the stuffing, heat the oil in a wok (*kadhai*); fry the potatoes till soft. Then add slices of bread and onions; sauté for a few minutes. Remove the wok from the heat and mix in the eggs.
- Slit the fish steaks horizontally and fill in the stuffing. Fold both sides of the steak in the centre. With the folded side facing down, refrigerate for a few hours or overnight.
- Steam the fish steaks in a colander over boiling water, when ready.
- For the tomato sauce, steam the tomatoes in a colander and remove when soft. When cool enough to handle, peel off the skin. Add onion juice, ginger and garlic pastes. Cook over medium flame till the consistency is sauce-like. Add salt, sugar and cream (if using). Put the steamed fish steaks in the hot sauce and serve.
- If desired, add the steaks to the tomato sauce when ready but still on the fire. Do not allow it to boil. This improves the flavour.

FISH A LA KIEV

PREPARATION TIME: 10 MIN.
COOKING TIME: 30 MIN.
SERVES: 4

Ingredients

500 gm Fish, deboned, cut into pieces
3 tbsp / 45 ml Refined oil
2 tbsp / 24 gm Onion, finely chopped
2 Green chillies, deseeded, chopped
¾tsp / 3 gm Salt
½ tsp / 1 gm Red chilli powder
½ tsp / 1 gm White pepper (*safed mirch*)
2 tsp / 10 ml Lemon (*nimbu*) juice
1 tbsp / 4 gm Green coriander (*hara dhaniya*), chopped
½ tsp / 1½ gm Sugar

For the sauce

1 tbsp / 20 gm Butter
1 tbsp / 10 gm Refined flour (*maida*)
¾ cup / 150 ml Milk
½ tsp / 2 gm Salt
a pinch Red chilli powder
White pepper (*safed mirch*)
2 Eggs, separated
1 tsp / 5 ml Vinegar or anchovy sauce
2 tbsp / 40 gm Butter
½ cup / 60 gm Breadcrumbs

Method

- Heat the oil in a pan; add the onions and sauté till light brown. Add green chillies, salt, red chilli powder, white pepper, lemon juice, green coriander, and sugar. Add fish and cook covered on low heat till fish is tender and the mixture is dry.

- For the sauce, melt the butter in a frying pan; add the flour and sauté for half a minute. Add the milk gradually, and cook till the sauce thickens. Add red chilli powder and white pepper. Remove from heat and beat in the egg yolks. Add vinegar or anchovy sauce.
- Add this sauce to the fish mixture and mix till well mashed. Refrigerate for a couple of hours, then divide the mixture into eight equal parts. Flatten each portion into a round. Place 5 gm of frozen butter in the centre of each. Shape into a pyramid by pulling the sides into a point.
- Dip each pyramid in egg whites and then coat with breadcrumbs. Refrigerate to harden. Remove.
- Heat the oil in a wok (*kadhai*); deep-fry the pyramids, a few at a time, till golden brown. Remove with a slotted spoon and drain the excess oil on paper towels. Serve at once.

A STICKY SOLUTION

TO REMOVE A FISH BONE STUCK IN YOUR THROAT GULP DOWN EITHER LEMON JUICE OR COOKED WHOLE RICE IMMEDIATELY.

SOLE FISH IN ORANGE JUICE

PREPARATION TIME: 30 MIN.
COOKING TIME: 30 MIN.
SERVES: 4

Ingredients

1 kg Sole fillets, deboned, skinned, washed, dried
1 Juice of lemon (*nimbu*)
Salt and black pepper (*kali mirch*) to taste
1 Egg
2 tbsp / 20 gm Seasoned refined flour (*maida*)

For the white sauce
4½ tbsp / 90 gm Butter
1 tbsp / 10 gm Refined flour
2 cups / 400 ml Milk
1 cup / 200 ml Orange juice
2 tsp / 10 gm Orange peel, shredded
a pinch Sugar

Method

- Marinate the fish in lemon juice and seasoning for ½ hour. Make a batter out of egg, flour, and seasoning. Dip the fish in batter and deep-fry till golden brown.
- For the white sauce, melt the butter in a pan; add the flour. When bubbles appear, remove from heat and add milk, gradually, stirring constantly. Return to heat and make a thick sauce. Season to taste.
- In a separate pan, gently heat the orange juice to which the peel has been added and cook for a minute. Add the juice and pour while hot over the fish. Garnish with a few peeled orange segments.

FISH CHOUX PIE

PREPARATION TIME: 10 MIN.
COOKING TIME: 15 MIN.
SERVES: 4

Ingredients

1 kg any river fish, washed, dried
1½ cups / 300 ml Milk
Salt and black pepper (*kali mirch*) to taste
2½ tbsp / 50 gm Butter
2 tbsp / 20 gm Refined flour (*maida*)
2 tbsp / 60 gm Cheese, grated

For the choux pastry
½ cup / 100 ml Water
3 tbsp / 60 gm Butter
7½ tbsp / 75 gm Refined flour
2 Eggs

Method

- Put the fish into a shallow pan with milk and a pinch of pepper. Cover the pan and simmer gently for 15 minutes until tender. Drain the liquid from the fish and make it up to ½ cup with extra milk.
- Melt the butter in a pan; add the flour. When small bubbles appear, remove from heat and gradually add the milk and ½ cup fish stock. Return the pan to the heat stirring constantly, till it thickens. Remove the pan from the heat. Remove the bones from the fish and stir the fish into the sauce with the cheese. Check the filling for seasoning before turning it into the dish.
- For the choux pastry, boil water and butter in a saucepan. Remove from heat and immediately add flour. Beat to a smooth paste that leaves the pan clean. Add eggs, one at a time, and beat until smooth and glossy.
- Pour the choux pastry over the filling and carefully spread the pastry to the sides. Bake in a preheated oven (150°C / 300°F) in the centre shelf for 30 minutes or until well risen and golden brown.

FISH FILLETS WITH MUSHROOMS IN MORNAY SAUCE

PREPARATION TIME: 1 HR.
COOKING TIME: 30 MIN.
SERVES: 4-6

Ingredients

1 kg White fish fillets, washed, dried
Salt to taste
3 tbsp / 45 ml Lemon (*nimbu*) juice

For the white sauce
1½ tbsp / 30 gm Butter
3 tbsp / 30 gm Refined flour (*maida*)
1 cup / 200 ml Milk
¾ tbsp / 15 gm Butter
200 gm Mushrooms, washed, chopped
½ tbsp Mixed herbs, chopped
Salt and black pepper (*kali mirch*) to taste
a pinch Mace (*javitri*), ground

For the mornay sauce
1½ tbsp / 30 gm Butter
2 tbsp / 20 gm Refined flour
1½ cups / 300 ml Milk
½ cup / 60 gm Cheese, grated
1 tsp / 2 gm Mustard powder
Salt and black pepper to taste
Croutons for decoration

Method

- Marinate the fish fillets in salt and lemon juice for ½-1 hour. Put in a pan and cook on simmer till tender.
- For the white sauce, melt the butter in a pan; add the flour and sauté. Gradually pour in the milk and stir continuously till the sauce thickens. This should produce half a cup of thick sauce.

- Heat the butter in another pan; sauté the mushrooms for a few minutes. Add mixed herbs, salt, black pepper, and mace; mix well.
- For the mornay sauce, melt the butter in a pan, add the flour and sauté. Pour in the milk stirring continuously till it comes to the boil. Cook till the sauce thickens to a cream-like consistency. Remove from heat and add cheese, mustard powder, salt, and black pepper.
- Reheat the mushroom mixture and spread down the centre of a serving dish. Arrange the fillets around the sauce, and coat with the mornay sauce.
- Mix 1 tbsp cream with a little grated cheese and pour on top of the mornay sauce. Put under a hot grill (180°C / 350°F) for 10 minutes.
- Serve immediately garnished with croutons.

FOR BONY PROBLEMS!

TWEEZERS ARE IDEAL FOR REMOVING SMALL BONES FROM FISH WHEN FILLETING.

FISH WITH TOMATO SAUCE

PREPARATION TIME: 2 HRS.
COOKING TIME: 20 MIN.
SERVES: 4

Ingredients

4 portions White fish, skinned, deboned
a few sprigs Parsley
2 Bay leaves (*tej patta*)
5 tbsp / 75 ml Olive oil / Refined oil
1 tbsp / 10 gm Seasoned flour
4-6 Garlic (*lasan*) cloves, crushed
500 gm Tomatoes, chopped
Salt and black pepper (*kali mirch*) to taste
a pinch Sugar

Method

- Lay the fish with herbs and bay leaves in a dish and pour the olive or refined oil all over. Leave for two hours, turning the fish once. Drain and dry the fish, then coat with the seasoned flour. Strain the marinade into a frying pan and when hot, fry the fish until golden on both sides and cooked. Drain the fish and keep hot. Add the garlic to the remaining oil in the frying pan and sauté until golden.
- Add the tomatoes and cook over high heat until the liquid is evaporated and the tomatoes are reduced to a purée. Season to taste and pour over the fish.

SIMPLE BAKED FISH

PREPARATION TIME: 15 MIN.
COOKING TIME: 30 MIN.
SERVES: 4

Ingredients

1 kg Fish, skinned, deboned, dried, cut into steaks
Salt to taste
1 Juice of lemon (*nimbu*)
2 tbsp / 40 gm Butter
Salt and black pepper (*kali mirch*) to taste
5 tbsp / 100 ml Cream

Method

- Marinate the fish in salt and lemon juice for 15 minutes.
- Arrange the fish on a greased fireproof dish; sprinkle some black pepper. Spoon over the cream and bake in a medium hot oven (150°C / 300°F) for about 30 minutes or till golden brown and tender.
- Serve hot.

BAKED FISH WITH ALMONDS

PREPARATION TIME: 6 MIN.
COOKING TIME: 40 MIN.
SERVES: 4

Ingredients

1 kg Sole or pomfret, cut into 4 portions
¼ cup / 30 gm Almonds (*badam*), roasted with skins removed
2 tbsp / 40 gm Butter, melted
1 Onion, minced
1 tbsp / 15 ml Lemon (*nimbu*) juice
1 Onion, sliced
2 Bay leaves (*tej patta*)
10 Black peppercorns (*sabut kali mirch*)
Salt and black pepper (*kali mirch*) to taste

Method

- Heat two tbsp hot water in a saucepan; add butter, almonds, and onion; simmer gently for five minutes. Remove from heat and add lemon juice.
- Place the sliced onion in a greased, shallow dish with the bay leaves and black peppercorns. Season the fish fillets with salt and black pepper and place over the onions. Cover with almond mixture and bake in a medium hot oven (150°C / 300°F) for 40 minutes or until tender.
- Serve hot.

SOLE FRIED IN BUTTER WITH ALMONDS

PREPARATION TIME: 15 MIN.
COOKING TIME: 20 MIN.
SERVES: 4

Ingredients

8 Sole fillets, washed, dried
Juice of 1 lemon (*nimbu*)
Salt to taste
1 tbsp / 10 gm Seasoned flour to dust
1¼ cups / 200 gm Butter
5 tbsp / 75 ml Refined oil
10 Almonds (*badam*), toasted in the oven, slivered
Parsley / Green coriander (*hara dhaniya*) / Mint (*pudina*) leaves, chopped for garnishing

Method

- Marinate the fillets in lemon juice and salt for 15 minutes. Then dust them with seasoned flour.
- Heat half the butter and all the oil in a pan; fry the fillets carefully till light brown. Remove from pan and keep hot.
- In the same pan add the remaining butter and heat till dark brown. Add a little lemon juice and remove from heat. Pour immediately over the hot fish, sprinkle the almonds and garnish with parsley or green coriander or mint.

FISH IN CUCUMBER SAUCE

PREPARATION TIME: 8 MIN.
COOKING TIME: 30 MIN.
SERVES: 4

Ingredients

8 Fillets of river fish, medium-sized, washed, dried
Salt and black pepper (*kali mirch*) to taste
2 Bay leaves (*tej patta*)
4-6 Curry leaves (*kadhi patta*)
8 Black peppercorns (*sabut kali mirch*)
½ cup / 100 ml Water
½ cup / 100 ml Milk

For the sauce
3 tbsp / 60 gm Butter
1 Cucumber (*khira*), diced
3 tbsp / 30 gm Refined flour (*maida*)
¾ cup / 150 ml Stock reserved from the fish
2 tbsp / 40 ml Cream

Method

- Season fish fillets with salt, pepper, and a dash of lemon juice. Roll them from the tail and place in a buttered fireproof dish with herbs and black peppercorns.
- Pour water over the rolled fish and cover with a lid. Either bake in an oven or cook over gentle heat for about 15 minutes or until tender. Remove fish, arrange on a serving dish and keep warm. Keep the fish stock for the sauce.
- For the sauce, melt butter in a pan; add cucumber and toss over gentle heat for a few minutes until lightly cooked. Remove and keep hot.
- Add flour to the same pan and sauté for a minute. Gradually blend in milk and fish stock, stirring continuously for two minutes. Remove the pan from heat and mix in cream and cooked cucumber. Check for seasoning.
- Pour sauce over the fish and serve hot garnished with cucumber and lemon slices.

HOTCH POTCH PIE

PREPARATION TIME: 15 MIN.
COOKING TIME: 30 MIN.
SERVES: 4

Ingredients

250 gm White fish, cooked
250 gm Potatoes, boiled, mashed
1 Egg, hard-boiled, chopped
1 tbsp Shrimps or prawns, cooked
1 tbsp Capers (optional)
Salt and black pepper (*kali mirch*) to taste
½ cup / 100 ml White sauce (see p. 96)
2 Tomatoes, medium-sized, cut into thin slices
2 tbsp / 30 gm Cheese, grated

Method

- Flake the fish and mix with potatoes, egg, shrimps, capers, salt, and black pepper. If not using shrimps or capers, increase the number of eggs.
- Turn the mixture into a greased pie dish and pour the white sauce over it.
- Garnish with tomatoes and cheese and bake in a medium hot oven (150°C / 300°F) in the centre shelf for about 30 minutes.

FISH STEAMED IN TOMATO SAUCE

PREPARATION TIME: 10 MIN.
COOKING TIME: 20 MIN.
SERVES: 4

Ingredients

8 Sole fillets or any good river fish, medium-sized
500 gm Tomatoes, chopped
Salt to taste
8 Black peppercorns (*sabut kali mirch*)
2 Bay leaves (*tej patta*)
½-1 cup / 100-200 ml Water
1 tbsp / 25 gm Onion, minced
2 Garlic (*lasan*) cloves, chopped
½″ piece Ginger (*adrak*), chopped
1 Green chilli
¾ tbsp / 15 gm Butter

Method

- Place all the ingredients in a pan, except the butter, and cook over gentle heat until the fish is tender. Remove the fish from the pan and keep hot.
- Cook the sauce further for a few minutes, until it is slightly thick. Strain, mix in the butter and pour over the fish.

SCALED OUT

TO REMOVE FISH SCALES EASILY RUB VINEGAR OVER THE SURFACE OF THE FISH.

FISH IN TOMATOES

PREPARATION TIME: 1 HR.
COOKING TIME: 20 MIN.
SERVES: 4

Ingredients

1 kg Fish, cut into medium-sized steaks
2 Juice of lemons (*nimbu*)
Salt to taste
½ cup / 100 gm Ghee
2 cups / 240 gm Onions, finely chopped
500 gm Tomatoes, finely chopped
1 tbsp / 4 gm Green coriander (*hara dhaniya*), chopped

Method

- Marinate the fish in lemon juice and salt for one hour.
- Heat the ghee in a pan; add the onions and sauté till dark brown. Add the tomatoes and a little salt. When slightly fried, add the fish. Keep turning the pieces from time to time. When the mixture becomes dry, and the oil comes to the surface, remove the pan from the heat.
- Serve garnished with green coriander and accompanied with bread rolls or steamed rice.

POMFRET IN MUSHROOM AND CHEESE SAUCE

PREPARATION TIME: 10 MIN.
COOKING TIME: 30 MIN.
SERVES: 6

Ingredients

6 Pomfret fillets, large, washed, dried
Juice of 1 lemon (*nimbu*)
Salt and black pepper (*kali mirch*) to taste
200 gm Button mushrooms, finely sliced
3 tsp / 15 gm Butter
1 cup / 200 ml Milk

For the sauce
1½ tbsp / 30 gm Butter
2½ tbsp / 25 gm Refined flour (*maida*)
1½ cups / 300 ml Milk
½ cup / 60 gm Cheese, grated
½ tsp / 1 gm Mustard powder
2 tbsp / 40 ml Cream

Method

- Marinate the fillets in lemon juice, salt and black pepper.
- Grease a large saucepan, lay the fillets on one side with the butter and mushrooms on the other side. Pour the milk over them. Cover, and cook gently on low heat, till tender. Strain the liquid and keep aside to use in the sauce. Separate the fish from the mushrooms and keep the fish warm in a dish.
- For the sauce, melt the butter in a pan; add the flour and sauté. Pour in the milk and the reserved liquid from the fish. Cook the sauce, stirring all the time, till it is the consistency of thin cream. Add the mushrooms and bring the mixture to the boil. Remove from heat; add the cheese, salt, pepper and mustard powder.
- Now add the cream and mix well. Pour the sauce over the fish. Serve immediately garnished with parsley.

CHINESE STEAMED FISH

PREPARATION TIME: 10 MIN.
COOKING TIME: 20 MIN.
SERVES: 4

Ingredients

8 Fish fillets, medium-sized
200 gm Mushrooms, finely sliced
4 Garlic (*lasan*) cloves, chopped
4 Spring onions, chopped with the greens, cut into 1″ pieces
6 tbsp / 90 ml Refined oil
½ tbsp / 7 ml Soya sauce
2 tsp / 4 gm Cornflour
3 tbsp / 45 ml White wine
Salt and black pepper (*kali mirch*) to taste

Method

- Place the fish and mushrooms in a large dish. Mix all the other ingredients well and pour over the fish.
- Steam the fish by placing the dish in a saucepan of boiling water. Cover the dish and steam for 15-20 minutes.
- Serve with rice or peas and potatoes.

FISH CROQUETTES

PREPARATION TIME: 10 MIN.
COOKING TIME: 30 MIN.
SERVES: 2

Ingredients

500 gm Singhara fish, washed
Salt and black pepper (*kali mirch*) to taste
2 Onions, sliced
1 Egg
a small piece of Ginger (*adrak*), minced
1 tbsp / 4 gm Green coriander (*hara dhaniya*), finely chopped
4-5 Mint (*pudina*) leaves, finely chopped
3 Garlic (*lasan*) cloves, minced
2 Green chillies, deseeded, minced
1 Egg, beaten
½ cup / 60 gm Breadcrumbs
Refined oil for frying

Method

- Place the fish in a pan with 1/4 cup of water. Add the salt, black pepper, and onions. Cook gently on low heat for 20 minutes or till well cooked. Mash and mix with the remaining ingredients.
- Divide the mixture equally into small portions. Shape each portion into croquettes. Dip the croquettes in egg, coat with breadcrumbs and deep-fry in hot oil till golden brown.
- Serve with steamed peas, carrots, and cauliflower.

FISH MOULD

PREPARATION TIME: 5 MIN.
COOKING TIME: 1 HR.
SERVES: 2

Ingredients

500 gm Fish
2 tbsp Green peas (*matar*), boiled
1 Tomato, sliced
1½ tbsp / 22 ml Vinegar (*sirka*)
3 tbsp / 60 gm Butter
1 sheet butter or waxed paper
1 tbsp / 10 gm Refined flour (*maida*)
1 cup / 200 ml Milk
2-3 Eggs
½ Lemon (*nimbu*) juice
Salt, pepper, red chilli powder to taste

Method

- Put the butter paper in a pan or mould and decorate the bottom with peas and tomatoes.
- Boil the fish in water, 1 tbsp vinegar, and salt.
- Make a white sauce with butter, flour and milk (see p. 96). Cook for a few minutes till it thickens. Cool slightly, add the eggs, lemon juice, remaining vinegar, and fish which has been mashed. Mix thoroughly, transfer contents in the prepared mould and steam.
- Invert on to a dish and serve garnished with lettuce leaves and tomatoes.

SHRIMPS ON RICE

PREPARATION TIME: 10 MIN.
COOKING TIME: 15-20 MIN.
SERVES: 6

Ingredients

1 kg Shrimps, shelled, deveined
2 tbsp / 30 ml Refined oil
2 Onions, small, chopped
1 cup / 200 ml Chicken stock (see p. 9)
4 tbsp / 100 gm Ginger (*adrak*), finely sliced
250 gm Green peas (*matar*), boiled
2-3 tsp / 4-6 gm Cornflour, dissolved in 4 tbsp water
1 tbsp / 15 ml Soya sauce
1 tsp / 4 gm Salt

Method

- Heat the oil in a pan; add the shrimps and onions. Use green spring onions, cut into 1″ pieces with the greens, if available. Cook until the shrimps turn pink, do not brown the onions. Add the stock, ginger, and green peas. Cook covered for a few minutes until the shrimps become tender.
- Remove the cover and stir in the cornflour and soya sauce. Cook until the sauce thickens slightly.
- Serve on a bed of steamed rice.

FISH KEBABS

PREPARATION TIME: 10 MIN.
COOKING TIME: 10 MIN.
SERVES: 4

Ingredients

500 gm Fish, deboned, steamed, mashed
1 Potato, large, boiled, mashed
1 Bread, slice, toasted, crushed
1-2 Green chillies, deseeded, finely chopped
1 tbsp / 4 gm Green coriander (*hara dhaniya*), finely chopped
Salt to taste

Method

- Mix all the ingredients together. Divide the mixture equally into small round kebabs.
- Heat the oil in a wok (*kadhai*); deep-fry the kebabs till golden brown. Remove with a slotted spoon and drain the excess oil on paper towels.
- Serve hot.

SOUR AND SALTY

LEMON JUICE TURNS BITTER IF KEPT FOR A LONG TIME. TO AVOID THIS, ADD A PINCH OF SALT TO IT.

BAKED FISH STEAKS

PREPARATION TIME: 10 MIN.
COOKING TIME: 55 MIN.
SERVES: 4

Ingredients

750 gm Fish steaks, boneless, cut into 1″ cubes
2 Capsicum (*Shimla mirch*), sliced
100 gm Button mushrooms
Salt to taste

For the white sauce
2½ tbsp / 50 gm Butter
5 tbsp / 50 gm Refined flour (*maida*)
1½ cups / 300 ml Fish stock (see p. 9)
1 Juice of lemon (*nimbu*)
Salt and black pepper (*kali mirch*) to taste
4 Tomatoes, quartered
Parsley, chopped, for garnishing

Method

- Place the fish in a baking dish with the capsicum, mushrooms, and salt.
- For the white sauce, melt butter in a pan; add the flour and sauté. Pour in the fish stock. Cook the sauce, stirring all the time till it is the consistency of thin cream. When the sauce is thick and smooth, add lemon juice and seasoning.
- Pour the white sauce over the fish and bake covered at 190°C / 375°F for 50 minutes or until the fish is tender. Ten minutes before cooking time, add the tomatoes. Serve garnished with parsley.

RUSSIAN SOURED FISH

PREPARATION TIME: 10 MIN.
COOKING TIME: 20 MIN.
SERVES: 4

Ingredients

8 Sole or haddock fillets
2 tbsp / 20 gm Seasoned flour (*maida*)
2½ tbsp / 50 gm Butter
1 tbsp / 15 ml Refined oil
100 gm Button mushrooms, sliced finely
1 tbsp / 10 gm Refined flour
1 cup / 200 ml Sour cream
¼ cup / 30 gm Cheese, grated
2 Eggs, hard-boiled, sliced
1 Lemon (*nimbu*), cut into slices
Tomatoes, cut into slices for garnishing

Method

- ▹ Toss the fish fillets in the seasoned flour.
- ▹ Heat the butter and oil in a pan; fry the fillets for 8-10 minutes. Remove and drain the excess oil thoroughly on paper towels.
- ▹ In the same oil, sauté the mushrooms until soft. Remove and drain. Stir in the flour into the remaining buttered oil and gradually add sour cream. Cook for a couple of minutes till the mixture thickens slightly. Add the cheese, mushrooms, and eggs.
- ▹ Arrange the fish on a hot platter and pour the sauce over it. Garnish with lemon and tomato.

VEGETABLES

SPINACH AND POTATO BAKE

PREPARATION TIME: 10 MIN.
COOKING TIME: 40 MIN.
SERVES: 2

Ingredients

500 gm Spinach (*palak*), washed
2 tbsp / 30 ml Refined oil
½ Onion, medium, finely chopped
4 Garlic (*lasan*) cloves, ground
1 Green chilli, deseeded, finely chopped
Salt and black pepper (*kali mirch*) to taste
250 gm Potatoes, boiled, mashed
2 cups / 400 ml Milk
1 tbsp / 20 gm Butter
1 tbsp / 10 gm Refined flour (*maida*)
3 tbsp / 45 gm Cheese, grated

Method

- ▹ Boil spinach without adding any water. When cool, grind and keep aside.
- ▹ Heat 1 tbsp oil in a pan; add onion and garlic; sauté till pink in colour. Add spinach, green chilli, salt and black pepper. Cook for a few minutes.
- ▹ Mix mashed potatoes with ½ cup milk. Add salt and pepper to taste.
- ▹ Melt the butter or half butter and half oil in another pan; add flour and sauté for a couple of minutes. Remove the pan from the heat and slowly add the remaining milk, beating continuously so that no lumps form. Add half the cheese, keep the rest aside for garnishing. Mix the sauce with the spinach mixture.
- ▹ Arrange the mashed potatoes in a greased baking dish. Spread the spinach mixture over the mashed potatoes. Sprinkle with the remaining cheese. If desired, add more cheese and dot with butter. Bake in a moderately hot oven (180°C / 350°F) for 20 minutes or till well browned.

Note: *If desired omit butter in the last step; instead, top with 1 tbsp double cream.*

MIXED VEGETABLES WITH OYSTER SAUCE

PREPARATION TIME: 8 MIN.
COOKING TIME: 10-15 MIN.
SERVES: 4

Ingredients

6 Baby corn (*bhutta*)
1 tbsp / 15 ml Refined oil
4-6 Garlic (*lasan*) cloves, finely chopped
2-3 Spring onions, cut into 1″-long pieces
1 Broccoli / Cauliflower (*phool gobi*), chopped into four pieces
2 Carrots (*gajar*), medium-sized
Salt and black pepper (*kali mirch*) to taste
1 Juice of lemon (*nimbu*)
1½ tsp / 7 ml Oyster sauce

Method

- Heat the oil in a pan; sauté the garlic for a few seconds. Add the spring onions and cook till soft.
- Now add the vegetables turn by turn according to their tenderness, and cook each vegetable for two minutes, before adding the next. Add black pepper and salt to taste.
- When ready, there should be some sauce left. Add lemon juice and oyster sauce; cook for a minute and serve hot.

Note: *To retain the green colour of broccoli either steam it for a minute or give two boils and remove.*

CABBAGE WITH BROCCOLI

PREPARATION TIME: 5 MIN.
COOKING TIME: 10 MIN.
SERVES: 2

Ingredients

½ Cabbage (*bandh gobi*), finely sliced
2 tbsp / 30 ml Refined oil
400 gm Broccoli
Salt to taste

Method

- Heat the oil in a pan; add the cabbage and stir-fry.
- Boil the broccoli for one minute to retain its colour and then steam until tender. Slice and mix with the cabbage. Season to taste and serve.

WONDER LEMON

TO RETAIN THE GREEN COLOUR OF THE LEAFY VEGETABLES USE A FEW DROPS OF LEMON JUICE.

POTATO CAKE

PREPARATION TIME: 10 MIN.
COOKING TIME: 1 HR.
SERVES: 6

Ingredients

1 kg Potatoes, peeled, finely sliced
3-4 tbsp / 45-60 ml Refined oil
2½ tbsp / 50 gm Butter
4 Garlic (*lasan*) cloves, minced
2 tbsp / 8 gm Parsley, fresh

Method

- Heat the oil in a large frying pan; add the potatoes and fry until just beginning to brown. It will take about half an hour. Season the potatoes.
- Grease an 8″ shallow, round, loose-bottomed tin with half the butter. Layer the potato slices in the tin, gently pressing it down. Bake at 150°C / 300°F for about half an hour or until brown. Remove from oven and spread the remaining butter around the inner edges of the tin.
- Transfer mixture on to a plate, browned side up. Sprinkle with garlic and parsley. Cut into wedges and serve.

SMELL-LESS

THE ODOURS OF CABBAGE OR CAULIFLOWER CAN BE MINIMISED BY ADDING A SLICE OF BREAD TO THE COOKING WATER.

STUFFED CAULIFLOWER WITH SPAGHETTI

PREPARATION TIME: 5 MIN.
COOKING TIME: 50 MIN.
SERVES: 6

Ingredients

1 kg Cauliflower (*phool gobi*), whole, cleaned
1 Onion, medium, sliced

For the white sauce
1¾cup / 75 gm Butter
5 tbsp / 50 gm Refined flour (*maida*)
2 cups / 400 ml Milk
½-1 cup / 100-200 ml Cauliflower stock (see below)
5 tbsp / 75 gm Cheese, grated
1 Egg, beaten

a pinch Cayenne pepper
Salt and black pepper (*kali mirch*) to taste
1 cup Spaghetti, boiled
a little Tomato sauce

Method

- Boil the cauliflower with the onion in enough salted water. Drain the water and keep aside.
- For the white sauce, melt the butter in a pan; add the flour and mix well. Gradually, pour in the milk and cauliflower stock, stirring continuously, so that no lumps form. Add 25 gm cheese and egg; mix well.
- Stuff cauliflower with the white sauce keeping some aside for the spaghetti. Sprinkle a little cheese, cayenne pepper and seasoning on top. Place the stuffed cauliflower in a greased baking tray and bake at 150°C / 300°F till the top of the cauliflower is light brown.
- Mix the remaining cheese sauce and tomato sauce with the spaghetti. Put the cauliflower in the centre of the serving dish and surround with the spaghetti. Serve garnished with boiled peas.

MIXED VEGETABLES WITH CHEESE SAUCE

PREPARATION TIME: 10 MIN.
COOKING TIME: 15 MIN.
SERVES: 4

Ingredients

150 gm French beans, fresh, stringed, cut into ½″ pieces
100 gm Button mushrooms
1 Cauliflower (*phool gobi*), medium
500 gm Green peas (*matar*), shelled, tender
a few stalks Asparagus

For the cheese sauce
2 cups / 400 ml Milk
3 tsp / 6 gm Cornflour
a pinch Salt
½ tsp / 1 gm Black pepper (*kali mirch*)
½ tsp / 1 gm Mustard powder
2 tbsp / 30 gm Cheese, grated

Method

- Poach the beans, half the mushrooms, and cauliflower carefully in salted water. Drain.
- Sauté the vegetables in butter for a few minutes. Arrange them in small portions on a hot platter.
- For the cheese sauce, make a cornflour paste with a little cold milk. Mix this with the milk. Cook on low heat till it thickens. Add seasoning. Cook for a minute. Add cheese and stir till the cheese melts, and the sauce is of pouring consistency.
- Pour the cheese sauce over the vegetables and serve.

VEGETABLE CHEESE CUTLETS

PREPARATION TIME: 20 MIN.
COOKING TIME: 20 MIN.
SERVES: 6

Ingredients

4 Potatoes, large, boiled, mashed

For the filling

2 tbsp / 30 ml Refined oil
1 tsp / 2 gm Cumin (*jeera*) seeds
1 tsp / 3 gm Mustard seeds (*rai*)
½ tsp / 1 gm Red chilli powder
1 tsp / 2 gm Garam masala
3 tsp / 6 gm Coriander (*dhaniya*) powder
1 tsp / 4 gm Salt
100 gm Carrots (*gajar*), finely chopped
100 gm French beans, finely chopped
100 gm Cauliflower (*phool gobi*), finely chopped
100 gm Cabbage (*bandh gobi*), finely chopped
100 gm Green peas (*matar*), shelled
¾ cup / 100 gm Cooking cheese, grated
1 Juice of lemon (*nimbu*)
a bunch Green coriander (*hara dhaniya*), chopped
2 Green chillies, deseeded, chopped
Refined oil for frying

Method

- For the filling, heat the oil in a heavy-bottomed pan; add the cumin and mustard seeds. When they splutter, add the spices and salt. Sauté for a few seconds and then add the vegetables and peas. Add enough water to cook the mixture. Remove from heat and add cheese. Keep this filling aside.
- Mix the mashed potato with salt, lemon juice, green coriander, and green chillies.

- Divide the potato mixture into 12 portions. Make a hollow in the centre of each portion and stuff 1 tbsp vegetable cheese mixture, seal the filling inside and shape into a cutlet. Coat them with breadcrumbs.
- Heat the oil in a pan; shallow-fry the cutlets till both sides are crisp and brown. Remove with a slotted spoon and drain the excess oil on paper towels.
- Serve hot with tomato chutney or sauce.

MILK WHITE

WHEN COOKING CAULIFLOWER, ADD 2 TBSP OF MILK TO RETAIN THE WHITENESS AFTER PREPARATION.

MACARONI WITH VEGETABLES

PREPARATION TIME: 10 MIN.
COOKING TIME: 15 MIN.
SERVES: 4

Ingredients

200 gm Macaroni
2 tbsp / 30 ml Refined oil
2 Onions, large, finely cut, lengthwise
4 Carrots (*gajar*), diced, boiled,
1 Potato, large, boiled, cubed
½ cup Green peas (*matar*), boiled
1 cup Cabbage (*bandh gobi*), shredded
1 cup Mushrooms, quartered, sautéed in a little oil, quartered
1 Tomato, chopped
Green coriander (*hara dhaniya*), finely chopped a small bunch
Salt to taste
2 tbsp / 30 ml Soya sauce
2 tbsp / 40 gm Butter

Method

- Boil the macaroni in salted water. Remove and pour some cold water to prevent sticking. Drain.
- Heat the oil in a pan; add the onions and sauté till golden brown. Add all the vegetables and cook for about five minutes or till tender.
- Add the macaroni and salt to taste, and keep stirring for another few minutes.
- Add soya sauce and butter; mix well. Remove from heat and serve hot.

VEGETABLE TERRINE WITH CHEESE SAUCE

PREPARATION TIME: 15 MIN.
COOKING TIME: 20 MIN.
SERVES: 6

Ingredients

1 Cabbage (*bandh gobi*), small, shredded
1 Cauliflower (*phool gobi*), small, cut into flowerets
1 Capsicum (*Shimla mirch*)
1 Red capsicum, cut into strips
2 Corn (*bhutta*) heads
250 gm French beans, stringed
500 gm Potatoes, peeled
500 gm Green peas (*matar*)
2 Aubergines (*baingan*), cut into rounds
a little Refined oil

For the sauce
2½ tbsp / 50 gm Butter
5 tbsp / 50 gm Refined flour (*maida*)
2 cups / 400 ml Milk
¾ cup / 100 gm Cheese, grated
Salt and black pepper (*kali mirch*) to taste

Method

- Boil the vegetables except the aubergines in enough water to cover. Add salt and cook till the vegetables are just tender and no water remains.
- Heat the oil in a pan; fry the aubergines till tender. Remove and drain the excess oil on paper towels.
- For the sauce, melt the butter in a pan; stir in the flour. Add the milk, gradually, and bring to the boil, stirring constantly. Cook for 10 minutes. Add cheese and seasoning. Pour into a shallow dish.
- Top with the vegetables and serve.

POTATOES BAKED WITH CREAM

PREPARATION TIME: 6 MIN.
COOKING TIME: 1 HR. 40 MIN.
SERVES: 4

Ingredients

500 gm Potatoes, cut into thick rounds
3-4 Garlic (*lasan*) cloves, peeled
3 tbsp / 60 gm Butter
Salt and black pepper (*kali mirch*) to taste
1 cup / 200 ml Cream

Method

- Rinse the potatoes thoroughly to remove the excess starch. Pat dry with a clean cloth then layer the potatoes in a shallow gratin dish which has been rubbed with garlic and greased with butter.
- After every layer, season lightly as you go along. Pour the cream over the mixture and dot with the remaining butter.
- Cover the dish with aluminium foil and cook in a preheated oven at 150°C / 300°F for about 1½ hours or until really tender.
- Remove the foil and increase the temperature to 190°C / 375°F for the last 10 minutes to get a golden crust.
- Serve hot.

SAY CHEESE!

CHEESE CAN BE KEPT FREE FROM FUNGUS BY PLACING A LUMP OF SUGAR IN THE CHEESE DISH. THE SUGAR ABSORBS MOISTURE AND KEEPS THE CHEESE FRESH.

BOMBAY BAKED BEANS

PREPARATION TIME: 6 MIN. PLUS OVERNIGHT
COOKING TIME: 2 HRS.
SERVES: 4

Ingredients

250 gm Dried white beans (*lobia*), soaked overnight, drained
3 tbsp / 45 ml Refined oil
2 Onions, large, peeled, chopped
1 Capsicum (*Shimla mirch*), chopped
500 gm Tomatoes, skinned, chopped
½ tbsp / 10 gm Jaggery (*gur*)
½ tbsp / 5 gm Refined flour (*maida*)
Salt and black pepper (*kali mirch*) to taste

Method

- Cook the beans in enough water to cover them. Bring to the boil and simmer for one hour or cook in the pressure cooker for 15 minutes. Drain (reserve the water to make the sauce).
- Heat two tbsp oil in a pan; add the onions and capsicum. Sauté for five minutes. Add tomatoes and jaggery; mix well. Cook covered over low heat.
- Meanwhile, heat the remaining oil in another pan; add flour and sauté over low heat. Pour in two cups of reserved water, stirring continuously, to make a thick sauce. Mix the sauce with the vegetable mixture and beans. Season to taste.
- Transfer contents into a shallow-greased casserole, bake at 180°C / 350°F for 1½ hours or until done.

STUFFED VEGETABLES

PREPARATION TIME: 20 MIN.
COOKING TIME: 1 HR. 40 MIN.
SERVES: 4

Ingredients

4 Tomatoes, large
4 Capsicum (*Shimla mirch*)
½ tsp / 1½ gm Sugar
4 tbsp / 60 ml Refined oil
1 Onion, medium, finely sliced
1 Aubergine (*baingan*), peeled, cubed
250 gm Rice, long-grained, soaked, drained, cooked
2 tbsp / 8 gm Mint (*pudina*) leaves / Dill, finely chopped
3 tbsp / 12 gm Parsley / Green coriander (*hara dhaniya*), chopped
1½ tbsp / 22 ml Tomato purée, diluted in 1 cup hot water
5 tbsp / 100 gm Butter, melted
½ tsp / a pinch Oregano / Carom seeds (*ajwain*)
Salt and black pepper (*kali mirch*) to taste

Method

- Cut a round from the top of the tomatoes and capsicum. Reserve the tops for sealing. Deseed the capsicum and scoop out the tomato flesh with a spoon. Chop and reserve for stuffing. Keep the tomatoes inverted to drain out the juice. Reserve the juice for the stuffing.
- Heat the oil in a pan; add the onion and sauté till brown. Add the aubergine and sauté together for a few minutes. Add the reserved tomato flesh and juice, rice, mint leaves or dill and parsley or green coriander; mix well.
- Fill the tomato and capsicum cups with the stuffing, seal with the tops and arrange them upright on a baking dish. Pour over the tomato purée, butter, and sprinkle oregano and seasoning. Cook in a preheated oven at 190°C / 375°F for 1½ hours, basting occasionally.
- This dish can be served hot or at room temperature.

GREEN BEAN CASSEROLE

PREPARATION TIME: 20 MIN.
COOKING TIME: 40 MIN.
SERVES: 4

Ingredients

500 gm French beans, fresh, stringed, halved, rinsed, drained
1¼ cup / 50 ml Refined oil
1 Onion, large, finely sliced
2-4 Garlic (*lasan*), cloves, finely sliced
1 Potato, peeled, cubed
400 gm Tomatoes, skinned, chopped
100 gm cheese, grated
Salt and black pepper (*kali mirch*) to taste

Method

- Heat the oil in a pan; sauté the onion and garlic until pale golden. Add the beans and potato; sauté together until well coated.
- Add the tomatoes and seasoning and cook for 30 minutes or until beans are tender, stirring occasionally.
- Sprinkle grated cheese on top and put under a hot grill for 10-15 minutes until the cheese has melted. Serve hot.

COOK TO PERFECTION!

VEGETABLES SHOULD ALWAYS BE COOKED UNTIL BARELY TENDER FOR A BETTER APPEARANCE, FLAVOUR AND TO RETAIN MORE FOOD VALUE THAN WHEN OVERCOOKED.

FRIED AND STUFFED AUBERGINES

PREPARATION TIME: 10 MIN.
COOKING TIME: 1 HR. 20 MIN.
SERVES: 4

Ingredients

500 gm Aubergines (*baingan*), rinsed
Ghee for frying
1 cups / 200 gm Onions, finely sliced
4 Garlic (*lasan*) cloves
250 gm Tomatoes, peeled, chopped
1 tsp / 2 gm Oregano
4 tbsp / 16 gm Parsley, finely chopped
Salt and black pepper (*kali mirch*) to taste
1 tsp / 5 ml Tomato purée, diluted in 1 cup hot water

Method

- Dry and slit the aubergines lengthwise like a pouch.
- Heat the ghee in a pan; fry the aubergines whole, turning them over and pressing them often on their slit sides until the inside is light golden. Remove and drain the excess oil on paper towels. Arrange the aubergines in a medium-sized oven dish and season.
- Sauté the onions in the remaining ghee until transparent. Add garlic and stir for a few minutes. Add tomatoes, oregano, parsley and seasoning; cook for 15 minutes.
- Fill the aubergine pouch with this sauce. Add the tomato purée and bake at 180°C / 350°F for 50 minutes to 1 hour, basting occasionally.

BAKED STUFFED POTATOES

PREPARATION TIME: 6 MIN.
COOKING TIME: 1 HR. 20 MIN.
SERVES: 4

Ingredients

4 Potatoes, large
½ cup / 60 gm Cooking cheese, grated
2 tsp / 12 gm Onion, finely chopped
2 tbsp / 40 gm Butter
Salt and black pepper (*kali mirch*) to taste
2-3 Tomatoes, ripe, firm, sliced

Method

- Scrub the potatoes well. Dry and prick all over with a fork. Then rub a little salt into the skins to make it crisp. Bake on the top shelf of the oven at 200°C / 400°F for about an hour. Remove and slit the potatoes into half lengthwise.
- Carefully scoop out the inside of the potato with a teaspoon leaving the skin intact like a shell.
- Mash the potato flesh lightly, then mix in the cheese (reserving a little), onion, butter, and a little milk. Season with salt and black pepper; mix well. Spoon the mixture back into the potato shells. Top each potato with the reserved cheese and a slice of tomato.
- Grill in the oven until the cheese has melted and is golden and bubbling.

CORN CROQUETTES

PREPARATION TIME: 10 MIN.
COOKING TIME: 10 MIN.
SERVES: 4

Ingredients

2½ cups Corn (*bhutta*) kernels, cooked
4 tbsp / 80 gm Butter
4 tbsp / 40 gm Refined flour (*maida*)
2 cups / 400 ml Milk
Salt and black pepper (*kali mirch*) to taste
2 tbsp / 8 gm Parsley, finely chopped
2-3 Egg yolks

For the coating

2 Egg whites, slightly beaten
1½ cups / 150 gm Seasoned flour
½ cup / 60 gm Breadcrumbs
Refined oil for frying

Method

- ▹ Melt the butter in a heavy-bottomed saucepan. Stir in the flour and cook for a few minutes until the mixture is pale gold in colour. Remove and pour in the milk, stirring constantly so that no lumps form. Return to heat and cook until the sauce thickens. Add salt and pepper to taste.
- ▹ Add the parsley, corn kernels, and egg yolks; mix well. The mixture should be of a thick dropping consistency. Remove and chill.
- ▹ Divide the mixture equally and shape each portion into croquettes. Dip in the beaten egg, roll over the flour and coat with breadcrumbs.
- ▹ Heat the oil in a pan; fry the croquettes, a few at a time, until heated through and crisp on the outside. Remove and drain on paper towels. Repeat till all are done.

Note: *For pure vegetarian croquettes you can omit the eggs.*

VEGETARIAN BOLOGNESE SAUCE

PREPARATION TIME: 10 MIN. – OVERNIGHT
COOKING TIME: 30 MIN
SERVES: 4

Ingredients

400 gm Pasta, wholewheat or spinach

For the sauce

1 cup / 100 gm Soya chunks
2 Bay leaf (*tej patta*)
2 tbsp / 30 ml Olive oil
1 Onion, chopped
4 Garlic (*lasan*) cloves, chopped
2 Carrots (*gajar*), chopped
2 Celery, chopped
1 Capsicum (*Shimla mirch*)
100 gm Mushrooms
500 gm Tomatoes, grated or blended
1-2 tbsp / 15-30 ml Tomato purée
2 tbsp / 30 ml Red wine (optional)
Salt and black pepper (*kali mirch*) to taste
Parmesan cheese, for garnishing

Method

- Boil the pasta in salted water with a few drops of oil for about nine minutes or till soft but not overcooked. Drain and keep aside.
- Heat the oil in a pan; sauté the onions and garlic until transparent. Add the carrots, celery and capsicum; cook for a further 2 minutes.
- Add the tomatoes, tomato purée, mushrooms, red wine (optional), soya chunks, bay leaf and salt and black pepper to taste. Simmer until the sauce is quite thick. Discard the bay leaf.
- Add the pasta and toss well.
- Serve hot topped with Parmesan cheese.

BROCCOLI TOMATO CHEESECAKE

PREPARATION TIME: 10 MIN.
COOKING TIME: 40 MIN.
SERVES: 4

Ingredients

300 gm Broccoli, florets
2 Tomatoes, large
2 cups Cottage cheese (*paneer*)
2 Eggs, separated
Salt and black pepper (*kali mirch*) to taste
a pinch Nutmeg (*jaiphal*)
½ cup Wholewheat biscuits crumbed
3½ tbsp / 70 gm Butter, melted
1 egg white for glaze

Method

- Steam the broccoli in boiling salted water until tender. Keep aside a few florets for garnishing.
- Immerse the tomatoes in boiling water for a minute; refresh in cold water, peel and deseed.
- Mash the cottage cheese with broccoli and tomatoes. Add the seasoning and egg yolks. Whisk the egg whites until soft peaks form. Fold into the mixture.
- Mix the biscuit crumbs and butter together, and press down well into a greased 22 cm quiche pan.
- Spread the filling over the base and bake for about 30 minutes or until slightly risen and just set. Remove.
- When cold, remove from pan and garnish with the remaining flowerets. Brush with egg white, if desired, and chill before serving.

VEGETABLE KIEV

PREPARATION TIME: 10 MIN.
COOKING TIME: 10 MIN.
SERVES: 4

Ingredients

500 gm Potatoes, peeled
1¼cups / 125 gm Refined flour (*maida*)
2½ tbsp / 50 gm Butter, cut into 1" squares
50 gm Green peas (*matar*)
1 cup / 100 gm Seasoned flour
2 Eggs, beaten
2 cups / 240 gm Breadcrumbs
Refined oil for frying

Method

- Boil the potatoes with a little salt. When the water dries up, add the flour and cook for 1 minute. Remove from heat. When cool, make a dough.
- Divide the dough equally into 6 portions. Make a hollow in the centre of each portion and stuff with green peas and a dollop of butter.
- Shape into a kiev (a triangular patty); roll in flour, dip in the egg and then coat with breadcrumbs. Repeat this process twice.
- Heat the oil in a frying pan; deep-fry the kievs till golden brown. Remove with a slotted spoon and drain the excess oil on paper towels.
- Serve hot.

STUFFED CAPSICUM

PREPARATION TIME: 5 MIN.
COOKING TIME: 50 MIN.
SERVES: 4

Ingredients

4 Capsicums (*Shimla mirch*), large
1 cup Leftover vegetable pulao or cooked mixed vegetables

Method

- Slice the top off the capsicums and deseed. Blanch for 2-3 minutes in boiling water. Drain.
- Fill the blanched capsicums with vegetable pulao or mixed vegetables. Place them in a dish and dot with butter.
- Bake in a moderately hot oven 180°C / 350°F for about 45 minutes or until tender. Serve with tomato sauce.

TOUGH KERNELS!

BOIL THE CORN KERNELS TILL TENDER; IF COOKED LONGER THEY BECOME TOUGH AGAIN.

GRILLED MUSHROOMS

PREPARATION TIME: 2 HRS.
COOKING TIME: 10 MIN.
SERVES: 4

Ingredients

500 gm Mushrooms, cleaned
¼ cup / 50 ml Olive oil
Salt and black pepper (*kali mirch*) to taste
4 Garlic (*lasan*) cloves, finely chopped
1 tbsp Chives or spring onion, finely chopped
1 tbsp Parsley, finely chopped
1-2 tsp / 5-10 ml Vinegar (*sirka*)

Method

- Marinate the mushrooms with oil, salt and pepper for a couple of hours. Remove and grill. Keep hot.
- Meanwhile, fry the garlic in the same oil in which the mushrooms were marinated. Add the chives or spring onions, parsely and vinegar; mix well. Pour the sauce over the grilled mushrooms.
- Alternately, cook the mushrooms with the marinade in a pan shaking the pan briskly. When done, add parsley and a generous squeeze of lemon.
- Serve hot.

NOODLE AND VEGETABLE CASSEROLE

PREPARATION TIME: 10 MIN.
COOKING TIME: 1 HR.
SERVES: 4

Ingredients

100 gm Noodles

For fresh tomato sauce
500 gm Tomatoes, large, red, roughly chopped
1 Carrot (*gajar*), chopped
1 Onion, small, chopped
2 Celery, finely chopped
2 Garlic (*lasan*) cloves, crushed
½ tsp / 1½ gm Sugar, ground
4 tbsp / 60 ml Refined oil
2 Onions, finely chopped
100 m French beans, finely sliced
1 Aubergine, finely chopped
2 Carrots, chopped into small pieces
6 Garlic cloves, crushed
2 Green chillies, deseeded, slit in half (optional)
Salt and black pepper (*kali mirch*) to taste
2 Capsicums (*Shimla mirch*), cut into strips
1¼ cups / 155 gm Cheese, grated

Method

- For the tomato sauce, cook all the ingredients in a saucepan and simmer gently until the tomatoes have puréed. Season to taste. Remove and strain the sauce.
- Heat the oil in a pan; fry the onions for 3 minutes. Add the French beans, aubergine, carrots, garlic, and green chillies; sauté for a minute.
- Add the prepared tomato sauce, salt and black pepper. Cover and simmer for about 8-10 minutes.
- Add capsicums just before removing from heat.
- Cook the noodles in boiling salted water till done. Drain and mix with the sauce; add cheese.
- Transfer contents into a casserole, cover and bake in a preheated oven at 150°C / 300°F for 30 minutes. Serve hot.

BABY POTATOES IN YOGHURT

PREPARATION TIME: 10 MIN.
COOKING TIME: 1 HR.
SERVES: 4

Ingredients

500 gm Baby potatoes, peeled
2 tbsp / 60 gm Yoghurt (*dahi*), thick
1 tbsp / 15 ml Water
a bunch Green coriander (*hara dhaniya*), chopped
1 tbsp / 18 gm Ginger-garlic (*adrak-lasan*) paste
Red chilli paste (optional)
¼ tsp Cumin (*jeera*) powder
¼ tsp Coriander (*dhaniya*) powder
2 tbsp / 30 ml Refined oil
Juice of 1 lemon (*nimbu*)

Method

- Prick the potatoes all over with a fork.
- Mix the yoghurt with the water.
- In a thick-bottomed pan, mix the potatoes with the rest of the ingredients (except the lemon juice) and half of the yoghurt and water mixture. Cook on medium heat till the oil floats on top and the spices are well cooked. Remove the pan from the heat.
- Transfer the contents into a baking tray and pour in the remaining yoghurt mixture. Cover the tray with an aluminium foil and bake in a moderately hot oven at 180°C / 350°F till the potatoes are done.
- Serve hot with a dash of lemon juice.

SPINACH-CHEESE SWISS ROLL IN MUSHROOM SAUCE

PREPARATION TIME: 10 MIN.
COOKING TIME: 50 MIN.
SERVES: 4

Ingredients

2 bunches Spinach (*palak*)
2 Eggs, beaten till fluffy
2½ tbsp / 50 gm Butter
7½ tbsp / 75 gm Refined flour (*maida*)
½ tsp / 3 gm Baking powder
Salt and black pepper (*kali mirch*) to taste
½ tsp / 1 gm Mustard powder
1 sheet butter paper

For the filling
1 tbsp / 15 ml Refined oil
1 Onion, small, chopped
½ tsp / 3 gm Garlic (*lasan*) paste
150 gm Cottage cheese (*paneer*)
½ cup / 60 gm Processed cheese
2 tbsp / 30 ml Milk
Salt and black pepper to taste

For the mushroom sauce
250 gm Tomatoes
1 tsp / 3 gm Sugar
4-5 Garlic cloves
1 tsp / 2 gm Cornflour, dissolved in a little water
200 gm Mushrooms, chopped

Method

- For the spinach roll, wash and boil the spinach in its own water. When cool, grind to a paste.
- Mix the butter, flour, baking powder, salt, black pepper, mustard powder, and spinach paste together.
- Grease a swiss roll pan and line it with butter paper. Pour the spinach mixture over it and bake in a moderately hot oven (180°C / 350°F) for about 30 minutes.

- Transfer the spinach roll with the butter paper on to a clean towel and roll while still hot. Keep aside to cool.
- For the filling, heat the oil in a pan; fry the onion and garlic paste for 2 minutes without browning. Add the cottage cheese, processed cheese, milk, and seasoning. Mix well.
- For the mushroom sauce, liquidize the tomatoes and strain through a sieve. Heat the tomato purée with sugar, seasoning, and garlic. Add cornflour and stir well.
- In a separate pan, sauté the mushrooms in oil for 4-5 minutes and add to the tomato mixture.
- Unroll the spinach roll, remove the butter paper, spread the filling over it and roll again. Pour the mushroom sauce over it.
- Serve garnished with cheese and accompanied with bread rolls.

EASY PEEL

TO PEEL TOMATOES EFFORTLESSLY AND WITHOUT A MESS, LEAVE THEM IN THE DEEP FREEZER OVERNIGHT. THE SKIN CRACKS ON ITS OWN.

STIR-FRIED VEGETABLES

PREPARATION TIME: 5 MIN.
COOKING TIME: 15 MIN.
SERVES: 4

Ingredients

3 cups Mixed vegetables, chopped
½ cup / 100 ml Vegetable broth (see p. 9)
1 tsp / 2 gm Cornflour
2 tbsp / 30 ml Refined oil
1 tsp / 6 gm Ginger (*adrak*), grated
1 Garlic (*lasan*) clove, chopped
½ cup / 60 gm Walnuts (*akhrot*), broken
1 Tomato, medium-sized, sliced
Salt to taste

Method

- Mix the cornflour with the vegetable broth.
- Heat the oil in a wok (*kadhai*); sauté the ginger and garlic for a few seconds. Add the mixed vegetables and fry for a few minutes. Remove and keep aside.
- In the same oil, fry the walnuts for a minute. Put the vegetables back in the wok and add the broth; mix well.
- Add the tomato and salt. Cook covered for a couple of minutes.
- Serve hot with steamed rice.

SALADS & DRESSINGS

MAYONNAISE

PREPARATION TIME: 20 MIN.
MAKES: 1 CUP

Ingredients

1 Egg
1 tsp / 2 gm Mustard powder
1 tsp / 3 gm Sugar
½ tsp / 2 gm Salt
1¼tsp Black pepper (*kali mirch*)
½ tsp Cayenne pepper
1 tbsp / 15 ml Lemon (*nimbu*) juice
1¼ cups / 250 ml Salad oil / Olive oil /Refined oil
1 tbsp / 15 ml Vinegar (*sirka*)

Method

- Blend the egg in an electric blender with mustard powder, sugar, salt, black pepper, cayenne pepper, and lemon juice. In the beginning add the oil slowly beating constantly till the sauce thickens, then add the oil faster.
- Gradually, add the vinegar. The sauce should be of a thick consistency. But if too thick, like double cream, thin it down with sour cream or fresh cream or yoghurt or milk or a little hot water.

QUICK MAYONNAISE

PREPARATION TIME: 20 MIN.
MAKES: ½ CUP.

Ingredients

1 Egg yolk
1 tsp / 5 ml Lemon (*nimbu*) juice
Salt and black pepper (*kali mirch*) to taste
½ cup / 100 ml Olive oil / Refined oil

Method

- Mix the egg yolk, lemon juice, and seasoning with a fork.
- Add the oil and beat with an egg beater. When the mixture begins to thicken add more oil, beating constantly. Flavour with lemon juice to prevent it from curdling.

Note: *All the ingredients: eggs, oil and even the bowl and mixer must be at room temperature. Warm the oil slightly if it has been refrigerated, rinse the bowl in hot or cold water and dry it before using.*

Mayonnaise was invented in 1756 during the reign of a great gourmet Louis XV of France when served by Duc de Richelieu, relative of the famed cardinal, who also bore that surname. Today mayonnaise is internationally known.

MAYONNAISE SAUCE

PREPARATION TIME: 20 MIN.
MAKES: 1 CUP.

Ingredients

2 Egg yolks
1 tsp / 4 gm Salt
½ tsp / 1½ gm Caster sugar
½ tsp / 1 gm Black pepper (*kali mirch*)
½-¾ cup / 100-150 ml Salad oil / Refined oil
2 tsp / 10 ml Vinegar (*sirka*)
1 tsp / 5 gm Mustard paste

Method

- Mix the egg yolks with salt, sugar, and black pepper with a wooden spoon.
- Add the oil, drop by drop, and stir well. When the mixture thickens a little, stir in the vinegar, also drop by drop.
- Add the mustard paste and mix well. The sauce when properly made must be as smooth and thick as double cream.

Variations: You can add 1 tsp Tabasco, 1 tsp onion juice, 1 tsp horseradish juice and tomato sauce to mayonnaise to make **Thousand Island Dressing**.

Tartar Sauce: add finely chopped onion, preferably spring onion; chopped green coriander, cucumber relish and if liked, a little more mustard to the mayonnaise. During the mango season, a little finely chopped raw mango can also be added.

Chaudfroid: is just mayonnaise and aspic jelly.

Mary Rose: is mayonnaise mixed with whipped cream and tomato sauce with a dash of Worcestershire sauce.

Aioli: is mayonnaise with garlic. It is usually served with fish, boiled vegetables or with boiled meat.

Green Mayonnaise: is mayonnaise mixed with the juice of green spinach leaves and finely cut celery leaves.

Note: *To toss salad correctly: Roll and toss the salad in a big bowl. Gently stroke downward to bottom with a salad fork in one hand and up and over with a salad spoon in the other hand. This down and over motion, with dressing delicately coating the greens, assures a salad of superb taste.*

LEMON STRIKES AGAIN!

SPRINKLE SOME LEMON JUICE OVER THE CUT APPLES TO KEEP THEM FROM DISCOLOURING.

SALAD DRESSING

PREPARATION TIME: 10 MIN.
MAKES: 1 CUP.
SERVES: 4

Ingredients

¾ cup / 150 ml Milk
¼ cup / 50 ml Vinegar (*sirka*)
1 tsp / 4 gm Salt
2 tsp / 4 gm Mustard powder
1 tbsp / 20 gm Sugar
1 tbsp / 10 gm Refined flour (*maida*)
½ tsp Cayenne pepper
2 Egg yolks, slightly beaten
1½ tbsp / 30 gm Butter, melted

Method

- Mix all the dry ingredients together.
- Add the egg yolks, butter, milk, and vinegar very slowly. Cook over boiling water until the mixture thickens. This dressing will keep for a few days bottled. Mix as required with a little sour or sweet cream.

APPLE SALAD

PREPARATION TIME: 20 MIN.
MAKES: ½ CUP.

Ingredients

2 Dessert apples, cored, chopped
1 Cabbage (*bandh gobi*), medium-sized, firm, preferably Savoy cabbage with a good heart, washed, dried, shredded
5 Celery, scrubbed, diced
a drop Milk

For the dressing
1 tbsp / 10 gm Refined flour (*maida*)
½ tbsp Mustard powder
½ tbsp Salt
1 tbsp / 20 gm Sugar
¾ cup / 150 ml Malt vinegar (*sirka*)
½ tbsp / 10-15 gm Butter
1 Egg
a pinch Black pepper (*kali mirch*)

Method

- Mix all the ingredients together. The red skins of the apples show brightly through the mixture.
- For the dressing, mix the flour, mustard powder, salt, and sugar together. Stir in just enough cold water to blend the ingredients.
- Add the vinegar and cook on low heat, stirring all the time. Beat well as the mixture comes to the boil, it will thicken rapidly. Simmer for a minute then take the pan off the heat and cool it slightly.
- Beat in the butter then the egg. Put this mixture into a bowl and place a piece of wet greaseproof paper over it to prevent a skin forming. When cold, cover and store in the refrigerator, till required. Add a little lemon juice before use.
- Pour the required amount of dressing over the apple salad, mix gently with a fork and serve.

FRUIT SALAD

PREPARATION TIME: 30 MIN.
SERVES: 4

Ingredients

2 Oranges, large, pared, remove pulp
3 Bananas, peeled, cut into ¼" pieces
400 gm Green grapes, halved
4 tbsp Walnuts (*akhrot*), chopped

For the dressing
2 Egg yolks, hard-boiled
½ tsp / 1 gm Mustard powder
Salt, pepper, sugar to taste
2 tbsp / 30 ml Water, cold
½ cup / 100 ml Cream, whipped or evaporated milk
½ tbsp / 7 ml Lemon (*nimbu*) juice

Method

- Mix all the fruits together in a bowl.
- For the dressing, blend the egg yolks with mustard powder, salt, pepper, sugar, and cold water. Continue to beat until the mixture is quite smooth. Add the cream or evaporated milk.
- Add lemon juice (do not add too much as the mixture will not rewhip afterwards).
- Add the dressing in the bowl; mix well.
- Cover with greaseproof paper and serve chilled on a bed of crisp lettuce leaves.

Variation: You can add chicken or ham pieces.

POTATO AND EGG SALAD

PREPARATION TIME: 15 MIN.
SERVES: 4

Ingredients

3 Potatoes, boiled, peeled, cut into rounds
1 tbsp / 15 ml Lemon (*nimbu*) juice
Salt and black pepper (*kali mirch*) to taste
French dressing (see p 136)
3 Eggs, hard-boiled, shelled, finely chopped
2 Tomatoes, firm
1 tsp /4 gm Mint (*pudina*) leaves, fresh, washed, dried, chopped

Method

- ▹ Mix all the ingredients together in a bowl.
- ▹ For the dressing, blend the egg yolks with mustard powder, salt, pepper, sugar, and cold water. Continue to beat until the mixture is quite smooth. Add the cream or evaporated milk.
- ▹ Add lemon juice (do not add too much as the mixture will not rewhip afterwards).
- ▹ Add the dressing in the bowl; mix well.
- ▹ Cover with greaseproof paper and serve chilled on a bed of crisp lettuce leaves.

Variation: You can add chicken or ham pieces.

CHICKEN AND PASTA SALAD

PREPARATION TIME: 30 MIN.
SERVES: 4

Ingredients

1 cup Chicken, boiled, deboned
½ cup / 100 ml Mayonnaise (see p. 128)
2 cups Macaroni, boiled, drained

For French dressing mix together

2 tbsp / 30 ml Malt vinegar (*sirka*) or half vinegar and half lemon juice
4 tbsp / 60 ml Olive oil / Refined oil
½ tsp / 1½ gm Sugar
½ tsp / 1 gm Mustard powder
¼ tsp / 1 gm Salt
¼ tsp / 1 gm Black pepper (*kali mirch*)
½ cup Spring onions, thinly sliced, diagonally
½ cup Mushrooms, chopped, sautéed in butter
1 Capsicum (*Shimla mirch*), julienned

Method

- Mix the chicken with the mayonnaise.
- Mix the macaroni with the French dressing.
- Arrange the salad leaves around the sides of a bowl. Put a layer of macaroni in the centre, then the chicken, again a layer of macaroni, mixed with spring onions. Garnish with mushrooms and capsicum. Chill covered for about 4-6 hours.

CHICKEN AND MIXED VEGETABLE SALAD

PREPARATION TIME: 30 MIN.
SERVES: 4

Ingredients

1 cup Chicken, boiled, deboned, diced
2 cups Mixed vegetables: capsicums (*Shimla mirch*), celery, carrots (*gajar*), spring onions, cauliflower (*phool gobi*)
1 egg, hard boiled
3 tbsp French dressing (see p. 136)

Method

- Mix all the ingredients together in a bowl.
- Add French dressing to taste and mix well. Cover the bowl and chill for a couple of hours before serving.

HOT POTATO SALAD

PREPARATION TIME: 30 MIN.
SERVES: 4

Ingredients

500 gm Potatoes, boiled, cubed
100 gm Bacon
1 Onion, diced
½ cup / 100 ml Mayonnaise (see p. 128)
1 tbsp Dill, finely chopped
½ tbsp / 2 gm Green coriander (*hara dhaniya*), finely chopped

Method

- Fry the bacon in its own oil until crisp. Remove and cut into pieces.
- Mix the bacon with the potatoes along with the bacon fat, onion and mayonnaise.
- Serve immediately garnished with dill and green coriander.

Variation: For hot potato salad with cheese, omit the bacon and add sautéed onion, tomato, capsicum and cheese to the boiled potatoes. Season to taste and serve.

APPLE AND VEGETABLE SALAD IN ORANGE SAUCE

PREPARATION TIME: 15 MIN.
COOKING TIME: 5 MIN.
SERVES: 4

Ingredients

2 Apples, red skinned, chopped, put in water to which lemon juice has been added to preserve the colour
1 Capsicum (*Shimla mirch*), large, julienned
¼ Cabbage (*bandh gobi*), small, fresh, julienned
1 Onion, small, finely sliced
2 Carrots (*gajar*), tender, sliced
1 Tomato, large, chopped

For the dressing

1 tbsp / 20 gm Sugar
2 tbsp / 30 ml Water
½ tsp / 1 gm Cornflour, dissolved in a little water
2 tsp / 10 gm Orange rind
Juice of 2 oranges
2 tbsp / 30 ml Salad oil
2 tbsp / 30 ml Vinegar (*sirka*)
1 tbsp / 15 ml Lemon (*nimbu*) juice
Salt and black pepper (*kali mirch*) to taste
a small piece Ginger (*adrak*), finely chopped
1 tsp / 3 gm Sesame (*til*) seeds, roasted
1 tsp Peanuts (*moongphalli*), chopped

Method

- Mix the fruit and vegetables (except the tomato) together in a large bowl
- For the dressing, cook the sugar and water together for 2-3 minutes. Add the cornflour paste and orange rind. Cook till the mixture thickens slightly. Remove from heat and cool immediately.
- Add the orange juice and mix thoroughly.
- In a separate bowl, mix the salad oil, vinegar, lemon juice, salt, black pepper, and ginger together. Mix this with the orange juice mixture. Pour over the apple and vegetable salad.
- Stir gently with a fork and serve in a glass bowl decorated with tomato, and sprinkled with sesame seeds and peanuts.

INDIAN SALAD

PREPARATION TIME: 15 MIN.
SERVES: 4

Ingredients

½ Cabbage (*bandh gobi*), small, finely shredded
Salt and black pepper (*kali mirch*) to taste
3 Potatoes, boiled, peeled, sliced
3 Tomatoes, large, sliced
3 Cucumbers (*khira*), small, peeled, sliced
2 Beetroot, boiled, peeled, cut into strips
2 tsp / 4 gm Mustard powder
1 tbsp / 15 ml Malt vinegar (*sirka*)
2 cups / 400 gm Yoghurt (*dahi*), thick
½ tsp / 1 gm Black cumin (*shah jeera*) seeds
1 tbsp / 4 gm Mint (*pudina*) leaves, chopped
½ cup / 12½ gm Green coriander (*hara dhaniya*), chopped
3 Green chillies, chopped

Method

- In a large salad bowl pile the cabbage in the centre. Add a little salt and black pepper. Arrange the potatoes in a circle around the cabbage.
- Arrange the tomatoes and cucumbers around the potatoes. Put half the beetroot on the tomatoes.
- Mix the mustard powder, one tsp vinegar, and yoghurt together. Add salt, black pepper, and black cumin seeds. Mix thoroughly and sprinkle half of it over the vegetables.

- Mix mint leaves, green coriander and green chillies together. Garnish the salad with green coriander mixture and the remaining beetroot. Pour the remaining yoghurt dressing and chill thoroughly before serving.
- Mix mint leaves, green coriander and green chillies together. Garnish the salad with green coriander mixture and the remaining beetroot. Pour the remaining yoghurt dressing and chill thoroughly before serving.

TOO MUCH TOO BAD

USE SALAD DRESSING AS MUCH AS REQUIRED AS TOO MUCH OF IT WILL OVERWHELM THE TASTE OF THE BASIC MEATS OR VEGETABLES IN THE SALAD.

SMOKED SALMON AND AVOCADO SALAD

PREPARATION TIME: 30 MIN.
SERVES: 4

Ingredients

200 gm Smoked salmon, thinly sliced
½ Cabbage (*bandh gobi*), finely chopped
1 Onion, small, minced
3 Carrots (*gajar*), medium-sized, coarsely grated
6 tbsp / 90 ml Mayonnaise (see p. 128)
100 gm Shrimps, cooked
6 Young salad leaves, washed, kept in chilled water for 30 minutes, dried
6 tbsp / 90 gm Cream cheese dip
1 Beetroot, grated, cooked
2 Avocados, medium-sized, peeled, diced

Method

- Mix the cabbage, onion, carrots with 4 tbsp mayonnaise. Cover and refrigerate.
- Mix the remaining mayonnaise with the shrimps.
- The salad leaves after drying curl up on the sides to look like a bowl. Divide the cabbage and shrimp mixture into 4 portions. On each salad leaf first put the cabbage mixture, then top with shrimps.
- Put the stuffed salad leaf on the top centre of the plate. Below it put 1 tbsp of cream cheese dip. On either side put a line of beetroot, flanked with avocados. On the bottom centre of the plate put the smoked salmon.

FISH SALAD

PREPARATION TIME: 10 MIN.
SERVES: 6

Ingredients

1 kg Fish, deboned, boiled, cubed
¾cup / 100 ml Mayonnaise (see p. 128)
¼ cup / 50 ml Orange juice
1 Juice of lemon (*nimbu*)
1-2 tbsp / 15-30 ml Tomato sauce
1 tsp / 5 ml Tabasco sauce
½ tbsp / 7 ml Worcestershire sauce
a few drops H.P. sauce
Salt and red chilli powder, if required
4 Eggs, hard-boiled, chopped
4 slices Pineapple, cut into smaller cubes than fish
1 Capsicum (*Shimla mirch*), deseeded, chopped
a few Lettuce leaves, chopped
1 tbsp / 4 gm Green coriander (*hara dhaniya*), chopped

Method

- Cool the salad bowl by placing it on a tray of ice. Add the mayonnaise and all the juices and sauces. Add seasoning, and mix well turning the bowl on the ice.
- Add the remaining ingredients mixing after each addition. Refrigerate for a couple of hours. Serve on a tray of ice.

CHICKEN AND PINEAPPLE SALAD

PREPARATION TIME: 8 MIN.
SERVES: 4

Ingredients

1 kg Chicken, boiled, cubed
4 Pineapple rings, chopped
1 cup / 200 ml Thousand island dressing (see p. 131)
1 Spring onion, finely chopped with its green tender leaves
a few Lettuce leaves
2 Carrots (*gajar*), peeled, grated

Method

- Mix all the ingredients together except the lettuce and carrots.
- Serve chilled on a bed of lettuce leaves and sprinkled with carrots.

EGG SALAD

PREPARATION TIME: 8 MIN.
SERVES: 4

Ingredients

12 Eggs, hard-boiled, halved
a few Mushrooms, finely chopped
3 tbsp Cottage cheese (*paneer*)
3 tbsp Chicken, boiled, shredded
Salt and black pepper (*kali mirch*) to taste

For the white sauce
1 tbsp / 20 gm Butter
2 tbsp / 20 gm Refined flour (*maida*)
1 cup / 200 ml Milk
Salt and black pepper to taste

Lettuce leaves, for garnishing
Tomatoes, chopped for garnishing
Celery, chopped for garnishing

Method

- Remove the egg yolks and soak the whites in cold water. Pass the egg yolks through a sieve, to break them up.
- Sauté the mushrooms in butter and remove.
- For the white sauce, heat the butter in a pan; add the flour and sauté for a minute. Remove the pan from the heat and gradually pour in the milk, stirring constantly so that no lumps form. Return to heat and cook till the sauce thickens. Divide the white sauce into three portions.
- Divide the yolks into three portions and mix one part with mushrooms, one part with cottage cheese, and one part with chicken.
- Add the white sauce in each mixture, and salt and pepper to taste. Remove the egg white from the water and cut into long strips; place in a bowl. Add the cottage cheese mixture, chicken mixture and finely the mushroom mixture.
- Serve garnished with tomatoes, lettuce, and celery.

CAESAR SALAD

PREPARATION TIME: 10 MIN.
SERVES: 6

Ingredients

3 Lettuce heads, medium, cut into 2-3″ width
½ cup / 100 ml Garlic olive oil (seep. 147)
2-3 tbsp / 30-45 ml Wine vinegar
1 Lemon (*nimbu*) juice
1 or 2 Coddled eggs, boiled in water for 2 minutes
Salt to taste
a dash Worcestershire sauce
Black peppercorns (*sabut kali mirch*), freshly ground to taste
6 tbsp / 90 gm Cheese, freshly grated
1 cup Caesar salad croutons (see p.147)

Method

- ▹ Place the lettuce leaves in a chilled salad bowl. Drizzle with garlic olive oil, vinegar, and lemon juice. Break in the eggs. Season with salt, Worcestershire sauce, and black pepper. Sprinkle cheese; roll and toss 6-7 times or till combined and till every leaf is coated.
- ▹ Add croutons, toss once or twice. Serve at once on chilled dinner plates. Garnish with rolled anchovies, if desired.

To make garlic olive oil: Add 6 sliced garlic cloves in 1 cup olive oil (you may use salad oil or half of each). Let the mixture stand for a while. Use as required.

To make Caesar salad croutons: Cut a slice of bread into 5 strips, length and breadthwise to make squares. Spread them out on a cooking sheet; pour a little garlic olive oil over the squares. Heat in an extremely slow oven (110°C / 225°F) for 2 hours. Croutons should be very dry so that they float in water. Sprinkle with grated cheese and store in an airtight jar; refrigerate.

DRESSING DOWN

IT IS UNWISE TO ADD CHOPPED TOMATOES TO A TOSSED SALAD, AS THEIR JUICES THIN THE DRESSING.

TUNA CREAM PUFF BOWL

PREPARATION TIME: 15 MIN.
COOKING TIME: 45 MIN.
SERVES: 4

Ingredients

For the cream puff bowl

¼ cup / 37 gm Butter
½ cup / 100 ml Boiling water
½ cup / 50 gm Refined flour (*maida*), sifted
½ tsp Celery seeds
2 Eggs

For the filling

4 Eggs, hard-boiled
30 gm Tuna, drained
1 tbsp / 15 ml Lemon (*nimbu*) juice
1 cup Celery, sliced
¼ cup / 30 gm Onion, finely chopped
½ cup / 100 ml Mayonnaise (see p. 128)
2 cups Lettuce, shredded

Method

- For the cream puff bowl, melt the butter in boiling water in a saucepan. Add the flour, celery seeds, and a dash of salt all at once, stirring vigorously. Lower heat and cook till the mixture forms a ball that does not separate.
- Add the eggs, one at a time, beating vigorously after each addition till smooth.
- Spread the butter mixture evenly over bottom and sides of a greased 9″ x 9″ pie plate. Bake in a very hot oven (230°C / 450°F) for 15 minutes, reduce heat to 170°C / 325°F and bake for 30 minutes more. Turn the oven off, keep the oven door closed and let the puff dry for about 20 minutes. Remove from oven and cool on the rack.

- For the filling, sieve one egg yolk and slice one whole egg. Keep aside for garnishing. Coarsely chop the remaining eggs.
- Break tuna in chunks and sprinkle with lemon juice. Add celery, onion, ¼ tsp salt, and a dash of pepper. Fold in the mayonnaise and remaining eggs; chill. Just before serving cover the bottom of the cream puff bowl with lettuce. Fill the bowl with tuna salad.
- Garnish with egg slices and sieved yolk.

WATER WORK

TO MAKE LETTUCE CRISP,
STAND IT IN WATER OVERNIGHT.

CREAM CHEESE AND POTATO ASPIC MOULD

PREPARATION TIME: 1 HR.
SERVES: 6

Ingredients

½ cup Capsicum (*Shimla mirch*), finely chopped
2 cups Carrots (*gajar*), finely chopped
1 Onion, finely chopped
500 gm Potatoes, boiled, peeled, diced
Salt to taste
½ tsp / 1 gm Black pepper (*kali mirch*)
1 tsp / 5 ml Chilli sauce
3 tsp / 15 ml French dressing (see p. 136)
1 tbsp / 15 gm Gelatin
¼ cup / 50 ml Water
1 cup / 200 ml Mayonnaise (see p. 128)
½ cup / 100 ml Cream
1 cup Cream cheese

Method

- Mix all the vegetables together in a bowl. Add salt, black pepper, and chilli sauce. Add the French dressing. Chill for an hour.
- Dissolve the gelatin in water thoroughly and add mayonnaise, cream, and cream cheese to it. Blend well with a fork and pour over the chilled vegetables; mix well with a spoon.
- Transfer the salad into a greased, chilled bowl and freeze for a few hours. Unmould when set and serve.

TUNA POTATO SALAD

PREPARATION TIME: 10 MIN.
SERVES: 6

Ingredients

2 Potatoes, medium-sized, boiled
2 tbsp / 30 ml Salad dressing
2 tbsp Parsley, snipped
3 cups Lettuce, torn
30 gm Tuna, drained, flaked
3 Eggs, hard-boiled
¾ cup / 90 gm Cheese, cut into strips
¼ cup / 30 gm Onion, finely chopped

For ½ cup salad dressing

⅔ cup / 135 ml Salad oil / Peanut oil
½ cup / 100 ml Malt vinegar (*sirka*)
½ cup / 100 ml Garlic (*lasan*) cloves, small, minced
1 tsp / 3 gm Caster sugar
¾ tsp / 3 gm Salt
1 tsp / 2 gm Mustard powder
Black pepper (*kali mirch*) to taste

Method

- Slice the potatoes into a salad bowl. Sprinkle 2 tbsp salad dressing and parsley; mix and chill. Then layer the remaining ingredients over the potatoes
- For the salad dressing, combine all the ingredients in a screw-top jar. Cover and chill for several hours. Shake well before use.
- Before serving, pour ½ cup dressing over the salad and toss lightly.

HAM AND POTATO SALAD

PREPARATION TIME: 1 HR.
SERVES: 6

Ingredients

2 cups Potatoes, boiled, cubed
1 tbsp / 15 ml Salad dressing (see p. 151)
1½ cups Ham, cubed, cooked
½ cup Cucumber (*khira*), diced, unpared
½ cup Radish (*mooli*), sliced
¼ cup Celery, chopped
¼ cup / 30 gm Onion, finely chopped
2 tbsp Capsicum (*Shimla mirch*), chopped
½ tsp / 2 gm Salt
½ cup / 100 ml Mayonnaise (see p. 128)

Method

- Mix the potatoes with the salad dressing in a salad bowl. Let it stand for one hour. Add the remaining ingredients except the mayonnaise; chill thoroughly.
- Before serving, gently fold in the mayonnaise.

SOAK TO DIGEST

SOAK CUCUMBERS IN SALT WATER FOR ABOUT AN HOUR OR TWO BEFORE USING. THIS WILL MAKE THEM MORE DIGESTIBLE AND THEY WILL ABSORB THE DRESSING MORE EASILY.

APPLE SALAD WITH A DIFFERENCE

PREPARATION TIME: 1 HR.
SERVES: 6

Ingredients

1 cup Red apples, diced, unpared
1 cup Golden apple, diced, unpared
1 Banana, large, peeled, sliced diagonally
1 cup Celery, sliced
½ cup / 60 gm Walnuts (*akhrot*), broken
½ cup / 50 gm Coconut (*nariyal*), flaked

For the dressing
¼ cup / 50 ml Mayonnaise (see p. 128)
1 tbsp / 20 gm Sugar
1 tsp / 5 ml Lemon (*nimbu*) juice
a pinch Salt
2 tbsp / 30 ml Cream, whipped

Method

- Combine the apples, banana, celery, walnuts, and coconut together.
- For the dressing, blend together mayonnaise, sugar, lemon juice, and salt. Fold in the whipped cream. Gently fold this into the apple mixture. Chill.
- Arrange the salad leaves in a bowl and spoon in the salad.
- Garnish with additional unpared apple slices and a sprig of mint.

TOSSED SALAD IN SOUR CREAM

PREPARATION TIME: 30 MIN.
SERVES: 8

Ingredients

1 cups Cabbage (*bandh gobi*), shredded
½ cup Celery, chopped
¼cup Capsicum (*Shimla mirch*), chopped
¼ cup Carrots (*gajar*), shredded
¼ cup Red radishes, sliced
¼cup Spring onion, sliced
2 tbsp / 40 gm Sugar
½ tsp / 2 gm Salt
½ cup / 100 ml Sour cream

Method

▹ Combine the first six ingredients together. Chill.
▹ Add the sugar and salt; mix well. Chill again.
▹ Just before serving, toss the sour cream mixture lightly with the vegetable mixture.

QUICK CHICKEN SALAD

PREPARATION TIME: 5 MIN.
SERVES: 4

Ingredients

2 cups Chicken, cooked, cubed
¼ cup Celery, diced
2 tbsp / 20 gm Raisins (*kishmish*)
½ cup / 100 ml Salad dressing of your choice
1 tbsp / 15 ml Lemon (*nimbu*) juice
Black pepper (*kali mirch*) to taste
½ tsp / 1 gm Curry powder
¼ cup / 30 gm Cashew nuts (*kaju*) / Peanuts (*moongphalli*)

Method

- Combine the chicken, celery, and raisins in a large bowl.
- Blend the salad dressing, lemon juice, salt, curry powder, and black pepper together. Toss lightly with chicken mixture. Chill.
- Before serving, add either cashew nuts or peanuts; toss well.

AVOCADO AND VEGETABLE TOSS

PREPARATION TIME: 10 MIN.
SERVES: 6

Ingredients

6-8 Corn cobs (*bhutta*), boiled, kernels removed
2 Avocados, medium-sized, peeled, diced
6 Eggs, hard-boiled, diced, chilled
2 tbsp / 24 gm Onion, chopped
1 cup / 200 ml Mayonnaise (see p. 128)
1 tbsp / 15 ml Lemon (*nimbu*) juice
½ tsp Chilli sauce
¼ tsp Cumin (*jeera*) seeds, ground
a little Nutmeg (*jaiphal*), grated

Method

- Combine the corn, avocados, eggs, and onion together in a bowl.
- Blend the remaining ingredients together.
- Mix the mayonnaise mixture lightly with the avocado mixture.
- Serve the salad on a bed of lettuce leaves.

DESSERTS

OVERNIGHT PUDDING

PREPARATION TIME: 10 MIN.
COOKING TIME: 2 HRS.
SERVES: 4

Ingredients

2 ¼ cups / 225 gm Self-raising flour (*maida*)
a pinch Salt
½ tsp Bicarbonate of soda
½ cup / 75 gm Butter
2½ tbsp / 50 gm Sugar
1 cup / 200 ml Boiling water
1 cup Mixed dried fruit
1 Egg, beaten

Method

- Sift the flour, salt, and bicarbonate of soda together. Rub in the butter and add the sugar.
- Pour the boiling water over the fruits.
- Add the egg and fruits along with the water to the flour mixture; beat well. Pour the mixture in a greased basin. Cover and leave overnight. The next day, steam the pudding. You can either steam in a steamer or put the basin covered in a big pan containing water. Cover the pan and bring the water to the boil. Then lower heat and simmer for two hours or till the pudding is done.

APPLE TART

PREPARATION TIME: 10 MIN.
COOKING TIME: 20-30 MIN.
SERVES: 4

Ingredients

500 gm Apples, peeled, sliced
2 Cloves (*laung*)
Sugar to taste

For the pastry
2 cups / 200 gm Refined flour (*maida*)
a pinch Salt
⅔ cup / 100 gm Butter
2 tbsp / 30 gm Breadcrumbs
2 tbsp / 30 ml Golden syrup

Method

- Stew the apples in a little water with the cloves. When soft, add the sugar. Keep aside to cool.
- For the pastry, sift the flour and salt together. Rub in the butter, and knead with enough water to make a smooth dough. Divide the dough into two portions and roll each out to the size of the baking tin. With one piece, line a greased tin. Sprinkle with breadcrumbs and add the golden syrup.
- Place the mashed apples on top. Cover with the remaining pastry. Prick well and bake for 20-30 minutes on the top shelf of the oven at 180°C / 350°F. Serve cold.

APPLE COBBLER

PREPARATION TIME: 10-15 MIN.
COOKING TIME: 30 MIN.
SERVES: 4

Ingredients

500 gm Cooking apples peeled, cored, sliced
½ cup / 75 gm Sugar
½ cup / 100 ml Orange juice
1 tbsp / 15 gm Marmalade

For the cobbler
½ cup / 50 gm Refined flour (*maida*) sifted
a pinch Baking powder
2½ tbsp / 50 gm Butter
2 tbsp / 40 ml Cream
a little Cold water

Method

- ▹ Mix the apples with half the sugar or according to taste, orange juice, and marmalade in a baking tin.
- ▹ For the cobbler, mix the flour with the baking powder. Rub in the butter till the mixture resembles breadcrumbs. Add the remaining sugar, cream and a little water and quickly mix till lumpy. Spread this over the apple mixture and bake for about 30 minutes or till brown. Serve warm.

BAKED CUSTARD WITH APPLES

PREPARATION TIME: 6 MIN.
COOKING TIME: 40 MIN.
SERVES: 4

Ingredients

4 Cooking apples, peeled, cored, sliced
1¼ tbsp / 25 gm Butter
Sugar to taste

For the custard
6 tsp / 18 gm Sugar
2 Eggs, separated
2½ cups / 300 ml Scalded milk

For the garnishing
1 or 2 Apples, peeled, cored, cut into rounds
a few Cherries
a little Sugar, preferably brown

Method

- Stew the apples in very little water till mashed; add the butter and sugar.
- For the custard, beat the egg yolks with sugar till smooth; add milk and mix thoroughly. Now add the slightly whipped egg whites and the mashed apples. Bake in a moderately hot oven (180°C / 350°F) for 30 minutes.
- When cooked, decorate with apples and cherries and sprinkle with brown sugar. Put under a hot grill for 10 minutes or till the apple is golden. Serve warm or cold.

JALEBI PUDDING

PREPARATION TIME: 1 HR.
COOKING TIME: 30 MIN.
SERVES: 4

Ingredients

500 gm Jalebis (available in most sweet shops)
4 cups / 800 ml Milk
3 Eggs

Method

- Soak the jalebis in milk for about an hour.
- Slightly beat the eggs and fold into the milk and jalebi mixture. Bake till cooked. Serve hot.

BEATING EGG WHITES - JUST RIGHT!

BEAT THE EGG WHITES WITH A PINCH OF SALT AND CREAM OF TARTAR FOR BEST RESULTS.

JAM ROLL

PREPARATION TIME: 10 MIN.
COOKING TIME: 30 MIN.
SERVES: 4

Ingredients

1 cup / 100 gm Refined flour (*maida*)
1 tsp / 6 gm Baking powder
¼ tsp / 1 gm Salt
3 Eggs, large
1 cup / 150 gm Sugar
⅓ cup / 65 ml Water
1 tsp / 5 ml Vanilla essence

For the Swiss Roll
4 tbsp Jam of your choice
Walnuts (*akhrot*) and raisins to taste
1 tbsp Icing sugar

Method

- Sift the flour, baking powder, and salt together.
- Beat the eggs until lemon coloured, gradually beat in the sugar, water, and vanilla essence till well mixed. Slowly mix in the dry ingredients. Do not over beat at this stage.
- Grease a rectangular pan and line with greased paper. Pour the batter into the pan and bake in a hot oven (190°C / 375°F) for 15-20 minutes.
- Loosen the edges and immediately turn upside down on a towel sprinkled with icing sugar. Remove the paper. While hot, roll the cake and the towel, cool on a rack.
- Unroll the cake, spread with softened jam and sprinkle with walnuts and raisins. Roll again. Sprinkle with icing sugar.

CRÊPE SOUFFLÉ

PREPARATION TIME: 10 MIN.
COOKING TIME: 30 MIN.
SERVES: 4

Ingredients

½ cup / 50 gm Refined flour (*maida*)
1 pinch Salt
1 Egg
1 Egg yolk
⅔ cup / 135 ml Milk
⅓ cup / 65 ml Cold water
a little Butter, melted

For the soufflé
1 tbsp / 20 gm Butter
1 tbsp / 10 gm Refined flour
1 cup / 200 ml Milk
1½ tbsp / 30 gm Sugar
1 Egg yolk
a little Liqueur (Cointreau) for flavour
2 Egg whites
a dash Lemon (*nimbu*) juice

Method

- Sift the flour and salt into a bowl. Add the egg and egg yolk and beat the mixture with a wooden spoon.
- Mix the milk and water together. Add ½ the liquid, gradually, to the flour mixture and mix continuously so that there are no lumps. When smooth, add the rest of the liquid and beat well; allow it to stand in a cool place for a while.
- Heat the oil in a non-stick frying pan; swirl it around, so that the bottom of the pan is well greased. Pour one tbsp batter and quickly swirl it around so that it spreads thinly on the base of the pan, cook for a minute, turn it over with a spatula, and cook the other side for another minute. Remove on to a hot plate. Make all the pancakes likewise. They can be frozen and kept.

- For the soufflé, melt the butter in a saucepan; add the flour and cook for a couple of minutes, stirring continuously.
- Meanwhile, boil the milk with the sugar and gradually stir into the pan. Cook for a few more minutes; stirring constantly. Remove from heat, cool slightly, then beat in the egg yolks and liqueur.
- Beat the egg whites till stiff and fold into the mixture.
- Arrange the pancakes on a baking sheet. On one half, spoon some of the soufflé and fold over. Cook in a hot oven (190°C / 375°F) for about 10 minutes or until the soufflé has risen and is cooked. Put the baked pancake on one side of the plate on which a little sugar syrup has been poured. On the other half of the plate decorate with a little mixed tinned or stewed fruit.

Note: *To make sugar syrup: mix together 100 gm sugar with ½ cup water and cook over low heat till the sugar dissolves. Then boil rapidly for five minutes and add a little lemon juice.*

KEEP THE INSECTS AT BAY!

TO KEEP REFINED FLOUR INSECT-FREE REFRIGERATE IN A POLYETHYLENE BAG.

AN EASY DESSERT

PREPARATION TIME: 1 HR.
COOKING TIME: 30 MIN.
SERVES: 6

Ingredients

200 gm Marie biscuits
1⅓ cup / 200 gm Butter
4 Eggs, separated
1 tin Condensed milk
3-4 Juice of lemons (*nimbu*), medium-sized
1 Cadbury chocolate, grated

Method

- Crush the biscuits and mix with slightly melted butter. Spread this mixture at the bottom and around the sides of a baking tin; refrigerate for an hour.
- Beat the egg whites till stiff and then gently mix in the yolks. Gradually fold in the condensed milk. When thoroughly mixed, add the lemon juice. Pour this mixture over the biscuit base.
- Sprinkle the chocolate on top and bake at 170°C / 325°F for 30 minutes. Transfer the contents into a serving dish.

APPLE SPONGE CAKE

PREPARATION TIME: 10 MIN.
COOKING TIME: 30 MIN.
SERVES:

Ingredients

2 Cooking apples, large, peeled, cored, grated
1 cup / 100 gm Refined flour (*maida*)
1 tsp / 6 gm Baking powder
a pinch Salt
¼ cup / 37 gm Butter
¼cup / 37 gm Caster sugar
1 Egg
a little Milk

Method

- Sift the flour, baking powder, and salt together.
- Beat the butter and sugar together. Add the egg and beat well. Add the flour mixture, a little at a time, and mix well. Whilst adding the flour, add a little milk from time to time, so that the mixture is of a dropping consistency. Pour into a greased pie dish.
- Sprinkle the apple over the sponge mixture with some lemon peel and orange juice or marmalade. Dredge liberally with caster sugar. Bake in a moderately hot oven (180°C / 350°F) for 30 minutes. Serve with cream.

SET CREAM DESSERT

PREPARATION TIME: 8 MIN.
COOKING TIME: 20-30 MIN.
SERVES: 6

Ingredients

2 tbsp / 30 gm Almonds (*badam*) unblanched
4 tbsp / 60 ml Water
1½ tbsp / 30 gm Sugar, ground

For the set cream
2½ cups / 500 ml Milk
½ cup / 75 gm Caster sugar
4 Egg yolks
1 tbsp / 15 gm Gelatin
4 tbsp / 60 ml Water
½ cup / 100 ml Double cream
2 Egg whites

Method

- Heat the sugar and water in a small pan. Cook on low heat till the sugar dissolves completely. Bring the syrup to the boil and boil rapidly until it is a mild golden brown.
- Stir in the almonds then pour the mixture on to a well-greased plate. Leave to set, then crush the mixture with a rolling pin.
- For the set cream, grease a mould large enough to hold four cups of liquid. Heat the milk slowly in a saucepan.
- Beat the sugar and egg yolks together in a bowl. Pour it in the hot milk, gradually, stirring all the time. Remove and strain the mixture and pour it back into the pan. Stir the custard mixture over gentle heat, without allowing it to boil, until it thinly coats the back of the spoon. Cool slightly and add the gelatine which has been dissolved in four tbsp of water.
- Stir in the crushed almonds. Pour the mixture into a bowl and leave

it until it is cold but not set. Whip the cream until fluffy but not stiff, and fold into the mixture. Beat the egg whites till stiff, mix a spoonful into the mixture then fold in the rest. Pour the mixture into the greased mould and leave to set.

- ▹ Turn the set cream on to a pretty dish and decorate with cream lightly whipped to spreading consistency to cover the top and sides thinly. Fill a piping bag with a plain writing pipe attached, with sieved red current jelly. Pipe straight lines an inch apart over the top of the cream. Draw the back of the knife across the lines, alternately from each side, at the same distance apart, making a feather pattern.

THIS OR THAT

GELATINE CAN BE SUBSTITUTED WITH CHINA GRASS. TAKE APPROXIMATELY TWICE THE QUANTITY OF THE REQUIRED GELATINE. (REFER TO THE INSTRUCTIONS ON THE PACKAGE.)

ORANGE CHIFFON PIE

PREPARATION TIME: 10 MIN.
COOKING TIME: 35 MIN.
SERVES: 6

Ingredients

150 gm Ginger biscuits or Marie biscuits
½ cup / 75 gm Unsalted butter, melted

For the filling
4 Eggs, separated
1 cup / 150 gm Sugar
1 cup / 200 ml Orange juice
¼ cup / 50 ml Lemon (*nimbu*) juice
1 tsp / 5 gm Orange rind
1 tsp / 5 gm Lemon rind
1 tbsp / 15 gm Gelatin, soaked in ¼ cup water
½ cup / 100 ml Cream, whipped

Method

- Crush the biscuits with a rolling pin, mix with the butter, and press into a 9″ spring or loose-bottomed cake tin. Chill.
- For the filling, beat the egg yolks and ½ cup sugar together in a bowl till cream coloured. Gradually, add the orange juice; mix well. Cook on low heat until it thickens. Remove and set to cool on ice.
- When semi-set, add the lemon juice, orange and lemon rind, which have been washed with boiling hot water and cooked for a couple of minutes with 1 tbsp sugar. Pour the mixture over the biscuit base.
- After soaking the gelatin in cold water for 15 minutes, then cook over boiling water, till the gelatin is fully dissolved. It is important to soak the gelatin in cold water until it softens.
- Beat the egg whites till frothy and gradually add ½ cup ground sugar. Fold in the gelatin and cream and pour over the orange pie. Decorate with orange flakes, mint leaves and cream.

EGGLESS CHOCOLATE SOUFFLÉ

PREPARATION TIME: 10 MIN.
COOKING TIME: 15 MIN.
SERVES: 6

Ingredients

2 sq Unsweetened chocolate
1 tbsp / 15 gm Gelatin
¼cup / 50 ml Cold water
½ cup / 75 gm Caster sugar
1 cup / 200 ml Milk
¾ cup / 112 gm Granulated sugar
¼ tsp / 1 gm Salt
2 cups / 400 ml Cream, thick

Method

- Melt the chocolate over boiling water.
- Sprinkle gelatin over cold water to soften.
- When the chocolate melts, stir in the caster sugar.
- Heat the milk until a thin film of cream shines on top, then stir in the chocolate mixture thoroughly. Cook stirring constantly, until the mixture reaches boiling point. Remove from heat and mix in softened gelatin, granulated sugar, and salt. Chill until thick as whipped egg white. At this point beat the mixture with a rotary or electric beater until light and airy- looking.
- In a separate bowl, beat the cream until very stiff. Fold the cream in the chocolate mixture and pour into a soufflé dish. Chill in the refrigerator until firm but spongy.

COLD COFFEE SOUFFLÉ

PREPARATION TIME: 10 MIN.
COOKING TIME: 20 MIN.
SERVES: 6

Ingredients

1 tbsp or 1 envelope Unflavoured gelatin
¼ cup / 50 ml Cold water
2 tsp / 10 gm Instant coffee
1 cup / 150 gm Sugar
½ tsp / 2 gm Salt
1 tsp / 5 ml Vanilla essence
4 Eggs, separated
1 cup / 200 ml Cream, heavy

Method

- Sprinkle gelatin over cold water to soften.
- Dissolve instant coffee in ½ cup sugar and salt on top of a double boiler. Cook over boiling water, stirring constantly, until slightly thick and custard-looking. Remove from heat, and stir in the gelatin mixture and vanilla essence; keep aside to cool.
- Beat the egg whites until stiff peak forms. Add the remaining sugar, gradually, and continue to beat until the mixture is shiny and stiff. Beat the heavy cream until it holds shape, then pile the cream on top of the egg whites and gently fold in the coffee mixture.
- Pour into a soufflé dish and chill for 3-4 hours or until firm but spongy. Can make overnight.

CHOCOLATE SOUFFLÉ

PREPARATION TIME: 10 MIN.
COOKING TIME: 20 MIN.
SERVES: 8

Ingredients

4 Eggs, large, separated
3 tbsp / 60 gm Sugar
3½ cups / 700 ml Milk
2 tbsp / 30 ml Cream
2 tsp / 10 gm Cocoa powder
4 tsp / 20 gm Gelatin
1 tsp / 5 ml Vanilla essence

Method

- Beat the egg yolks and sugar till thick and creamy. Whip the egg whites till stiff; keep aside.
- Boil the milk, add cream and mix well. Remove from heat and pour in the egg yolk mixture. Return to heat and cook on low heat till the mixture coats the back of a wooden spoon. Add cocoa powder, which has been previously mixed in a little cold milk, to the hot custard.
- Add gelatin dissolved in ½ cup milk and ½ cup water. Allow it to stand for 20 minutes. Place the mixture over ice and stir constantly. When the mixture is chilled and beginning to set, fold in the stiffly beaten egg whites.
- Pour into a glass dish and refrigerate overnight.

TANGERINE SNOW

PREPARATION TIME: 1 HR.
SERVES: 6

Ingredients

1 tbsp / 15 gm Gelatin
1 cup / 200 ml Boiling water
¼ cup / 37 gm Sugar
2 tsp / 10 ml Lemon (*nimbu*) juice
1 cup / 200 ml Orange juice, fresh
1 Egg white
¼ cup / 50 ml Cold water

Method

- Sprinkle gelatin over cold water to soften. Add boiling water, sugar, lemon and orange juice. Stir thoroughly.
- Cool in refrigerator until thick as unbeaten egg whites, then beat with a rotary or electric beater until frothy and pale cream in colour.
- Beat the egg white until soft peaks form, fold in the orange mixture gently and pour into six individual glasses. Chill in the refrigerator for one hour or more until firm but still spongy.

ORANGE DELICIOUS PUDDING

PREPARATION TIME: 10 MIN.
COOKING TIME: 50 MIN.
SERVES: 6

Ingredients

2½ tbsp / 50 gm Butter
½ cup / 75 gm Caster sugar
2 Eggs, separated
1 cup / 100 gm Refined flour (*maida*)
1 tsp / 6 gm Baking powder
1 Finely grated rind and juice of orange
1 cup / 200 ml Milk
a little Icing sugar for dredging

Method

- Cream butter and sugar together till light and fluffy. Add egg yolks and beat with a wooden spoon.
- Sift the flour and baking powder together. Add the flour mixture, orange rind and juice. Gradually, add the milk, stirring well. (Don't worry if the mixture curdles as it will make its own sauce during cooking.)
- Whisk the egg whites till stiff. Lightly fold into the mixture with a metal spoon. Transfer the mixture into a greased ovenproof dish and stand the dish in a large pan containing cold water. Bake in a moderately hot oven (180°C / 350°F) for about 40 minutes or till well risen, golden and cooked.
- Dredge with icing sugar and serve hot with cream (optional).

APPLE JOY

PREPARATION TIME: 8 MIN.
COOKING TIME: 1 HR.
SERVES: 4

Ingredients

2 Cooking apples, large, peeled, cored, grated
1 cup / 100 gm Refined flour (*maida*)
¼cup / 37 gm Caster sugar
1 Egg
a few drops Milk
1 tsp / 6 gm Baking powder
¼ cup / 37 gm Unsalted butter
a pinch Salt

For the rum sauce
1-2 Egg yolks
¼cup / 37 gm Caster sugar
¼ cup / 50 ml Rum
1-2 tsp / 5-10 ml Lemon (*nimbu*) juice
½ cup / 100 ml Cream, whipped

Method

- Mix all the ingredients together (except the apples) to a dropping consistency. Pour the mixture into a greased pie dish. Spread the apple over the mixture.
- Dredge liberally with caster sugar. Bake for 30 minutes in a moderately hot oven (180°C / 350°F).
- For the rum sauce, beat the egg yolks and sugar till a pale cream colour. Add rum and lemon juice. Add cream, mix well.
- Serve with rum sauce or whipped cream (optional).

PARADISE PIE

PREPARATION TIME: 10 MIN.
COOKING TIME: 45 MIN.
SERVES: 6

Ingredients

⅔ cup / 100 gm Sugar
1⅔ cups / 250 gm Butter
2 Eggs
5 cups / 500 gm Refined flour (*maida*)
½ tsp / 3 gm Baking powder
a little Sour cream, (if not available, add a little lemon juice to fresh cream)

For the stuffing
5 cups / 1 lt Milk
7 tbsp / 70 gm Refined flour
2⅔ cups / 400 gm Sugar
1⅔ cups / 250 gm Butter
100 gm Chocolate, grated

Method

- Beat the sugar and the butter till light and fluffy. Add the eggs, one by one, and beat after each addition.
- Sift the flour and baking powder together. Add to the sugar mixture. Work in the flour with your hands. Add the sour cream and mix well. Roll out the dough to the size of the baking tin and bake in a moderately hot oven (180°C / 350°F) for 30 minutes. Remove and leave to chill in the refrigerator. This stops the pastry from shrinking.
- For the stuffing, bring the milk to the boil. Add flour mixed with a little cold milk. Lower heat and cook till thick and like custard. Remove and stir till it cools.
- Beat the sugar and butter together. Add the chocolate. Now mix the milk mixture with the butter mixture. Beat again. Pour this mixture over the pastry. Refrigerate for 2-3 days. Then cut into pieces and serve.

QUICK DESSERT

PREPARATION TIME: 6 MIN.
COOKING TIME: 30 MIN.
SERVES: 4

Ingredients

500 gm Pears, ripe, peeled, cored, cut into cubes
3 tbsp / 60 gm Unsalted butter
½ cup / 75 gm Caster sugar
2 tbsp / 30 gm Ghee / Refined oil
2 tbsp / 20 gm Semolina (*suji*)
3-5 cups / 750-ml - 1L Milk
4 tbsp / 120 gm Sugar
2 tbsp / 30 gm Custard powder, dissolved in ¼ cup cold milk
1 Lemon (*nimbu*) rind, grated
1 tsp / 5 ml Vanilla essence
1 tbsp / 20 ml Cream

Method

- Keep the pears in a bowl of salted water.
- In a heavy-bottomed frying pan, melt a little more than half the butter on low heat. Sprinkle half the sugar, moving it around so that the pan is coated. Add the pears. Cook for about 10 minutes on moderate heat. Turn over the pear cubes, dot with rest of the butter and sprinkle the remaining sugar. Cook over low heat for another 10 minutes until golden.
- Melt the ghee or oil in a heavy pan; add the semolina and cook till a pleasant aroma emanates. Be careful not to brown it. Add the milk and bring to the boil. Add the sugar and custard powder mixture; keep stirring continuously till the mixture thickens. Add the lemon rind, vanilla essence, and cream. Keep beating the custard till it cools and looks smooth and fluffy.
- Remove the pears on to a serving dish and pour the custard on top. Decorate with a few cherries or chopped nuts. Serve cold or hot.
- You can sprinkle brandy or Cointreau, or serve with ice cream or whipped cream.

SEMOLINA CREAM

PREPARATION TIME: 5 MIN.
COOKING TIME: 20 MIN.
SERVES: 6

Ingredients

10 cups / 2 L Milk
2½ tbsp / 50 gm Sugar
2 tbsp / 20 gm Semolina (*suji*)
1 tsp / 5 ml Vanilla essence
¼tsp Nutmeg-green cardamom (*jaiphal-choti elaichi*), ground
Cherries or walnuts (*akhrot*) and raisins (*kishmish*), chopped for garnishing

Method

- Cook the milk, sugar and semolina on low heat till thick. Remove from heat, add vanilla essence, and nutmeg-green cardamom powder; mix well.
- Served garnished with cherries or walnuts and raisins.

SCORCH-FREE

TO KEEP MILK FROM SCORCHING, RINSE THE PAN WITH HOT WATER.

MIXED FRUIT DESSERT IN LEMON SAUCE

PREPARATION TIME: 10 MIN.
COOKING TIME: 10 MIN.
SERVES: 6

Ingredients

2 Apples, peeled, cored, chopped in cubes mixed with lemon juice to prevent discolouring
3 Bananas, sliced, mixed with lemon juice
1 cup Pineapple, cubed
20 Strawberries, hulled, halved
4 cups Grapes, halved

For the sauce
¼cup / 50 ml Lemon (*nimbu*) juice
¼cup / 37 gm Sugar

4 Strawberries, whole with caps and leaves for decoration
a few sprigs Mint (*pudina*) leaves

Method

- Mix all the fruits together in a glass bowl.
- For the sauce, mix the sugar with ½ cup water and boil till thick. Remove and cool. Then mix in the lemon juice and pour over the fruits and decorate with whole strawberries, a few grapes and mint leaves.
- Serve chilled with ice cream or whipped cream.

FRIED APPLES AND BANANAS IN BUTTER

PREPARATION TIME: 5 MIN.
COOKING TIME: 30 MIN.
SERVES: 4

Ingredients

2 Apples, peeled, cored, cut into quarters
1½ tbsp / 30 gm Brown sugar
½ tsp / 1 gm Cinnamon (*dalchini*) powder
2 tbsp / 40 gm Butter
2 Bananas, ripe, peeled, cut in half lengthwise

For the lemon curd
2½ tbsp / 50 gm Butter
⅔ cup / 100 gm Sugar
3-4 Juice of lemons (*nimbu*), strained
2 tsp / 10 gm Lemon rind, grated
2 Eggs

Method

- Roll the apples in brown sugar mixed with cinnamon powder.
- Melt the butter in a pan; fry the apples. Remove the apples to a dish. In the same pan, put a little more butter, and slightly fry the bananas. Decorate them round the apples.
- For the lemon curd, melt the butter on top of a double saucepan with the water boiling slowly underneath. Add the sugar, lemon juice and rind; stir until the sugar dissolves completely.
- Beat the eggs slightly and stir into the mixture. Keep stirring until it thickens and coats the back of a wooden spoon. When ready, pour into smaller warmer jars and cover immediately. Keep well in the refrigerator for about a couple of months.
- Serve with 1 tbsp lemon curd spread over the fried bananas.

APRICOT AND MANGO CREAM

PREPARATION TIME: 5 MIN.
COOKING TIME: 10 MIN.
SERVES: 4

Ingredients

150 gm Apricots
2 Mangoes, large
1 tbsp / 15 ml Water
2 tbsp / 40 gm Sugar

½ cup / 100 ml Double cream
1 tbsp / 15 ml Honey
2 tbsp / 60 gm Yoghurt (*dahi*), thick
1 tsp / 5 ml Lemon (*nimbu*) juice

Method

- Stew the apricots in water; add the sugar. Cook till the apricots are tender and no liquid remains.
- Blend all the ingredients in an electric blender till smooth. Spoon into individual glass bowls. Decorate with walnut halves and serve chilled.

GOING BANANAS!

BANANAS WILL STAY FRESH FOR A FEW DAYS IF STORED IN AN AIRTIGHT CONTAINER IN THE REFRIGERATOR.

VANILLA ICE CREAM

PREPARATION TIME: 6 MIN.
COOKING TIME: 2-3 MIN
SERVES: 3

Ingredients

2 Eggs, separated
3 tbsp / 60 gm Sugar
1 cup / 200 ml Milk, hot
½ cup / 100 ml Cream, whipped
1 tsp / 5 ml Vanilla essence

Method

- Whip the eggs yolks and sugar together till pale yellow in colour. Pour in the hot milk, stirring constantly. Cook till a thin custard is made.
- Add cream and stir well. Remove and let the mixture cool in ice water. Add vanilla essence.
- Whip the egg whites till soft peaks form. Fold the whipped egg whites into the mixture. Pour into a covered tray and freeze. Once or twice during the first hour of freezing it should be taken out and stirred briskly with a fork.

NOUGAT ICE CREAM

PREPARATION TIME: 5 MIN.
COOKING TIME: 5 MIN.
SERVES: 3

Ingredients

1 cup Walnuts (*akhrot*) and almonds (*badam*)
¾ cup / 112 gm Sugar
½ cup / 100 ml Cream, heavy, lightly whipped
2 tbsp / 40 gm Icing sugar
2 Egg whites, stiffly beaten

Method

- Caramalize the sugar in low heat, stirring constantly. Add the walnuts and almonds; mix thoroughly. Remove immediately and spread on a greased plate.
- Break the caramalized walnuts and almonds into pieces with a rolling pin.
- Mix the cream with the sugar and nuts. Lastly, fold in the egg whites into the cream. Pour into a tray and freeze.

MANGO ICE CREAM

PREPARATION TIME: 5 MIN.
COOKING TIME: 1 HR.
SERVES: 3

Ingredients

3 cups / 600 ml Milk
2½ tbsp / 50 gm Sugar
½ cup / 100 ml Cream
1 large or 2 medium sized Mangoes, pulped

Method

- Cook the milk in a pan till reduced to 2 cups. Add the sugar and cream and cook for a few more minutes. Remove from heat and cool to room temperature.
- Now add the mango pulp and mix thoroughly. Pour into a tray and freeze for 2 hours.

Note: *You can avoid using cream, by using just the custard made with eggs and sugar and frozen. To stop crystals from forming, use a little cornflour.*

PEACHES WITH CHOCOLATE

PREPARATION TIME: 5 MIN
SERVES: 2

Ingredients

1 Swiss roll (see p. 163)
4 Peaches, tinned, halved
4 tbsp / 60 ml Cream, thick, whipped
4 tbsp / 120 gm Yoghurt (*dahi*), well beaten or hung yoghurt
2 thick slabs Chocolate, grated

Method

- Place the Swiss roll in individual serving plates and moisten with a little peach syrup. Top with chopped peaches, chill.
- When ready to serve, fold the cream into the yoghurt and pour on top of the peaches. Decorate with chocolate.

PLUMS AND STRAWBERRIES WITH SOUR CREAM

PREPARATION TIME: 5 MIN.
COOKING TIME: 20 MIN.
SERVES: 4

Ingredients

200 gm Plums, stoned
100 gm Strawberries, hulled, halved
3 tbsp / 45 ml Sour cream, fresh
2 tbsp / 40 gm Sugar
4 tbsp / 60 ml Water
3 tsp / 9 gm Brown sugar for decoration

Method

- Mix the sugar in water and cook gently, stirring continuously, till the sugar dissolves completely. Increase the heat and boil rapidly for a couple of minutes. Remove from heat and cool.
- Mix the plums with the strawberries. Transfer on serving plates and pour the sugar syrup on top.
- Spoon the sour cream over the fruits and decorate with brown sugar. Serve chilled.

SOME HOUSEHOLD HINTS

* To make brass sparkle, use lemon rind, salt, and a little washing powder.
* Salt sprinkled on soot or fresh ink prevents stains on the carpets.
* Salt sprinkled on carpets during sweeping brightens the carpets and keeps the moths away.
* Salt sprinkled on stoves over spilled fat prevents a foul odour.
* To remove solidified wax from the candle holders easily, place them in a freezer for an hour or so. The wax will peel off easily.
* To prevent moth damage, put a few whole cloves in woollen clothes and pockets of sweaters.
* To prevent dampness in cupboards make holes in the plastic lid of a tin filled with charcoal and keep it in the bottom shelf. Or wrap and hang 12 chalk pieces.
* To remove dampness in a room place blocks of camphor in each corner of the damp room. The camphor will disappear, so will the dampness.
* To remove grass stains on flannels use kerosene, alcohol, lemon juice or two parts of ammonia to one of warm milk.

* To remove grime on knife blades, rub some raw cut potato over the knife.
* Greenfly on plants can be destroyed by spraying with a solution of borax: 30 gm to a litre of water.
* Beauty does not lie in creams and lotions alone. In fact, natural healthy beauty comes only from natural beauty aids. Here are some common recipes that are time tested for lasting loveliness:
* **Gram flour** (*besan*): is good for refining and cleaning the skin. Make a paste with one tablespoon gram flour and some water; apply over face and neck. Rub gently, then wash off.
* **Mint** (*pudina*) **Juice**: is good for blemishes and pimples. Extract the juice from a handful of mint leaves and apply over the entire face every night before going to bed. In the morning wash your face with water. This lotion eases away pimples and blemishes and makes the skin petal soft. Must be done regularly for a month for best results.
* **Watermelon Juice**: Grate and squeeze the juice from a small piece of watermelon; apply on face for about 15 minutes, then wash with warm water and splash with cold water. This lotion freshens the skin and also clears the skin of all blemishes.
* **Tomato Juice**: To one tablespoon of tomato juice add a couple of drops of lemon juice. Mix well and apply over face, keep on for half an hour, and then wash face with ordinary tepid tap water. This lotion is very effective in shrinking enlarged pores.

INDEX

Fish & Other Seafood

Vegetarian

Salads & Dressings

Desserts